I0020427

Microsoft Dynamics NAV Development Quick Start Guide

Get up and running with Microsoft Dynamics NAV

Alexander Drogin

BIRMINGHAM - MUMBAI

Microsoft Dynamics NAV Development Quick Start Guide

Copyright © 2018 Packt Publishing

All rights reserved. No part of this book may be reproduced, stored in a retrieval system, or transmitted in any form or by any means, without the prior written permission of the publisher, except in the case of brief quotations embedded in critical articles or reviews.

Every effort has been made in the preparation of this book to ensure the accuracy of the information presented. However, the information contained in this book is sold without warranty, either express or implied. Neither the author, nor Packt Publishing or its dealers and distributors, will be held liable for any damages caused or alleged to have been caused directly or indirectly by this book.

Packt Publishing has endeavored to provide trademark information about all of the companies and products mentioned in this book by the appropriate use of capitals. However, Packt Publishing cannot guarantee the accuracy of this information.

Commissioning Editor: Richa Tripathi
Acquisition Editor: Siddharth Mandal
Content Development Editor: Smit Carvalho
Technical Editor: Leena Patil
Copy Editor: Safis Editing
Project Coordinator: Pragati Shukla
Proofreader: Safis Editing
Indexer: Tejal Daruwale Soni
Graphics: Alishon Mendonsa
Production Coordinator: Tejal Daruwale Soni

First published: December 2018

Production reference: 1261218

Published by Packt Publishing Ltd.
Livery Place
35 Livery Street
Birmingham
B3 2PB, UK.

ISBN 978-1-78961-276-9

www.packtpub.com

`mapt.io`

Mapt is an online digital library that gives you full access to over 5,000 books and videos, as well as industry leading tools to help you plan your personal development and advance your career. For more information, please visit our website.

Why subscribe?

- Spend less time learning and more time coding with practical eBooks and videos from over 4,000 industry professionals

- Improve your learning with Skill Plans built especially for you

- Get a free eBook or video every month

- Mapt is fully searchable

- Copy and paste, print, and bookmark content

Packt.com

Did you know that Packt offers eBook versions of every book published, with PDF and ePub files available? You can upgrade to the eBook version at `www.packt.com` and as a print book customer, you are entitled to a discount on the eBook copy. Get in touch with us at `customercare@packtpub.com` for more details.

At `www.packt.com`, you can also read a collection of free technical articles, sign up for a range of free newsletters, and receive exclusive discounts and offers on Packt books and eBooks.

Contributors

About the author

Alexander Drogin started working with Navision Attain version 3.01 in 2002 as a software developer at a consulting company. After seven years of development, he shifted his focus to end-user support. In 2012, he joined the Microsoft Russia development team as a software engineer in testing, and worked on NAV test automation and sustained engineering tasks. He currently works as a NAV technical architect for a Microsoft partner in Malta.

About the reviewer

Oleg Romashkov has been a NAV developer since 2001. He has worked for Microsoft for 10 years, developing new features and country localizations for NAV 4.00-NAV 2019. Also, he spent seven years working for a few Microsoft partners, where he implemented NAV for more than 30 customers' projects.

Packt is searching for authors like you

If you're interested in becoming an author for Packt, please visit `authors.packtpub.com` and apply today. We have worked with thousands of developers and tech professionals, just like you, to help them share their insight with the global tech community. You can make a general application, apply for a specific hot topic that we are recruiting an author for, or submit your own idea.

Table of Contents

Preface   1

Chapter 1: Getting Started with the NAV Development Environment   7
  Installing the NAV development environment   8
    Setup configuration   8
    License information   10
  Managing NAV server configuration with Microsoft Management
  Console (MMC)   10
    Creating a NAV server instance with MMC   10
    Modifying server settings with MMC   13
    Connecting to the new server instance   14
  Managing NAV installation with NAV the Administration Shell   15
    Creating a NAV Server instance with Administration Shell   15
    Managing the NAV server with the Administration Shell   16
  Introducing the Object Designer   17
    C/SIDE and application objects   17
    Hello World example   20
    Running objects from the Object Designer   21
  Exporting and deploying NAV objects   21
    Managing objects with the Dynamics NAV Development Shell   23
  Summary   26

Chapter 2: Codeunits - Structuring C/AL Code   27
  Compiling a codeunit and error handling   27
    Handling compilation errors   28
  Declaring and calling functions   29
  Function parameters and return values   30
    How to add parameters to a function   31
    Function return value   32
  Declaring variables – variable scope   33
    Local variables   33
    Variable properties – declaring arrays   34
    Global variables   37
  Passing variables by value and by reference   38
  Record variables   41
    Iterating over a recordset   41
    Filtering records   43
    Inserting and modifying records   45
  Codeunit variables – calling functions from other codeunits   46
  Text constants   50

Summary 51

Chapter 3: Tables - Creating Data Structure 53
  Designing the table structure 53
    Creating tables 54
    Synchronizing table metadata with SQL Server 56
  Defining the primary key and secondary indexes 58
    Defining primary keys 58
    Table indexes 59
  Configuring default pages for tables 60
    Creating a list page using a page wizard 60
    Configuring default lookup and drilldown pages 61
  Table relations 62
  Field class – Flowfields and Flowfilters 65
    Modifying FieldClass 65
    Configuring the field calculation formula 66
    Adding a field to a page 68
  Table triggers 69
  Rec and xRec global variables 73
  Summary 75

Chapter 4: Designing User Interface 77
  Page creation wizard 78
    Card pages 78
    List pages 80
  ListPart and CardPart pages – subpages and FactBoxes 82
    ListPart subpage 82
    FactBox subpages 85
  Page triggers – C/AL code in pages 90
  Lookups and DrillDowns 94
  Page action designer 96
  Menu suite 100
  Summary 105

Chapter 5: Exchanging Data with XML Ports 107
  Importing data from CSV files 107
  Importing data from XML files 111
  XMLport triggers 113
  Exporting table data 119
  Designing the request page 121
  Running XMLports from C/AL code 124
    Exporting data from a C/AL function 125
    Importing XML from C/AL 127
  Summary 128

Chapter 6: NAV Event Model   129
Integration events   130
Database trigger events   135
UI events   142
Publishing custom events   145
    Event publisher function   146
    Raising events   147
Manual event subscription   149
Summary   154

Chapter 7: Presenting Data in Reports   155
Preparing a report dataset   155
Modeling a report layout   159
    Layout design   160
    Formatting data output   165
Report triggers   167
Designing a report request page   170
RDLC expressions   172
Interactive reports   174
Data items based on temporary tables   176
Summary   180

Chapter 8: Debugging Your Code   181
Activating the debugger   181
Breakpoints   183
    Activating breakpoints   183
    Break rules   184
Conditional breakpoints   185
Variables – Watches – Callstack   186
Capturing code coverage   188
Summary   190

Other Books You May Enjoy   191

Index   195

Preface

This book will introduce Microsoft Dynamics NAV - C/SIDE to the reader. It will give an overview of the internal system language and the most essential development tools. The book will enable the reader to customize and extend NAV functionality with C/AL code, design user interfaces through pages, create role centers, and build advanced reports in Microsoft Visual Studio. Readers will learn how to extend a NAV data model, write and debug custom code, and exchange data with external applications.

Microsoft Dynamics NAV is a modern ERP system covering most companies' needs for information. Out of the box, it comes with a rich set of application modules that provide functionality in different functional areas, ranging from accounting to manufacturing and servicing.

Still, the variety of business processes is much wider than any single ERP system can comprehend. To meet all the needs of companies that choose Dynamics NAV as their ERP software, it provides customization capabilities with its built-in development environment. The NAV - C/SIDE environment allows you to tailor your application to your needs by changing base code or adding your own extensions.

This book introduces the reader to the application development tools provided by Microsoft Dynamics NAV. You will learn how to work with the NAV database, organize code in code libraries, develop a user interface, and exchange data with external data sources. The book also gives an overview of the NAV event model, explaining development practices that allow modifications to the functionality without changing the base application code.

Reports are a natural part of any corporate information system. The ability to present aggregated data in an easily readable format is what is always required from an information system. A separate chapter of the book is dedicated to the reporting capabilities of NAV and its report editor.

Who this book is for

This book is for experienced users of Microsoft Dynamics NAV who have some experience of programming, but who may not be familiar with the NAV development environment or its internal development language, C/AL.

What this book covers

Chapter 1, *Getting Started with the NAV Development Environment*, introduces the NAV development environment. It also covers the installation and basic setup and familiarizes the readers with the object designer interface.

Chapter 2, *Codeunits – Structuring C/AL Code*, explains how to create a Codeunit, which is a container for C/AL code. You will write your first Client Application Language (C/AL) function and learn the foundations of the NAV C/AL.

Chapter 3, *Tables – Creating Data Structure*, describes main elements of the user interface—pages, page controls and actions, menus, and role centers. You will design simple card, list, and document pages to present different types of data, create role centers tailored to individual set of tasks performed by each user role, and customize page appearance and behavior with C/AL code.

Chapter 4, *Designing User Interface*, explains that NAV table objects are mapped to database tables stored in a SQL Server database. The data model is based on tables that store users' data. This chapter describes structure of tables – fields, primary keys, secondary indexes, and table relations. It also gives introduces table triggers, where developers can put their code to handle database triggers, such as record insertion or modification.

Chapter 5, *Exchanging Data with XML Ports*, describes XMLports—objects intended to import data received from external sources and export NAV data into CSV and XML files. XMLport is a quick and easy way to describe a hierarchical data structure and save it into a file. This is a common method of generating XML reports for external reporting systems.

Chapter 6, *NAV Event Model*, explains that Microsoft Dynamics NAV presents an extensible event model that allows developers to alter a system's behavior in a non-intrusive way. You will learn how to create custom objects that can be invoked automatically by the NAV platform or business application in response to certain events.

Chapter 7, *Presenting Data in Reports*, explains how to create visual reports in a report designer step by step, from a simple static list to an interactive report that supports sorting and filtering.

Chapter 8, *Debugging Your Code*, is an overview of the debugging capabilities of C/SIDE development environment. Readers will be introduced to step-by-step code execution, breaking the code execution process at certain points and under specified conditions. You will learn tips and tricks that will help you to quickly catch and fix programming errors in the C/AL code.

To get the most out of this book

Reader of the book should be familiar with Microsoft Dynamics NAV from the user perspective. System entities, such as documents, journals, and dimensions, come without explanation. It is good if you have basic understanding of computer programming. Deep knowledge of software development principles is not required, but it is assumed that the readers know what functions and variables are, and are aware of fundamental database concepts, such as tables, fields, indexes, and relations.

Download the example code files

You can download the example code files for this book from your account at www.packt.com. If you purchased this book elsewhere, you can visit www.packt.com/support and register to have the files emailed directly to you.

You can download the code files by following these steps:

1. Log in or register at www.packt.com.
2. Select the **SUPPORT** tab.
3. Click on **Code Downloads & Errata**.
4. Enter the name of the book in the **Search** box and follow the onscreen instructions.

Once the file is downloaded, please make sure that you unzip or extract the folder using the latest version of:

- WinRAR/7-Zip for Windows
- Zipeg/iZip/UnRarX for Mac
- 7-Zip/PeaZip for Linux

The code bundle for the book is also hosted on GitHub at https://github.com/PacktPublishing/Microsoft-Dynamics-NAV-Development-Quick-Start-Guide . In case there's an update to the code, it will be updated on the existing GitHub repository.

We also have other code bundles from our rich catalog of books and videos available at https://github.com/PacktPublishing/. Check them out!

All compiled objects from the book source also available on GitHub, you can run them with the demo license of Microsoft Dynamic NAV.

Conventions used

There are a number of text conventions used throughout this book.

`CodeInText`: Indicates code words in text, database table names, folder names, filenames, file extensions, pathnames, dummy URLs, user input, and Twitter handles. Here is an example: "The `MESSAGE` function is used to display a UI message."

A block of code is set as follows:

```
OnRun()
MESSAGE('Hello World');
```

When we wish to draw your attention to a particular part of a code block, the relevant lines or items are set in bold:

```
PROCEDURE CreateSalesInvoice(VAR LeaseContractHeader : Record 50500) :
Code[20];
VAR
  SalesHeader : Record 36;
BEGIN
  OnBeforeCreateInvoice(LeaseContractHeader);
  CreateSalesInvoiceHeader(SalesHeader,LeaseContractHeader);
  CreateSalesInvoiceLines(SalesHeader,LeaseContractHeader."No.");
  OnAfterCreateInvoice(LeaseContractHeader,SalesHeader);
  EXIT(SalesHeader."No.");
END;
```

Any command-line input or output is written as follows:

```
Get-Command -Module Microsoft.Dynamics.Nav.Management,
Microsoft.Dynamics.Nav.Apps.Management
```

Bold: Indicates a new term, an important word, or words that you see onscreen. For example, words in menus or dialog boxes appear in the text like this. Here is an example: "If for some reason the database does not open automatically, choose the **Database** | **Open** option from the **File** menu."

Warnings or important notes appear like this.

Tips and tricks appear like this.

Get in touch

Feedback from our readers is always welcome.

General feedback: If you have questions about any aspect of this book, mention the book title in the subject of your message and email us at customercare@packtpub.com.

Errata: Although we have taken every care to ensure the accuracy of our content, mistakes do happen. If you have found a mistake in this book, we would be grateful if you would report this to us. Please visit www.packt.com/submit-errata, selecting your book, clicking on the Errata Submission Form link, and entering the details.

Piracy: If you come across any illegal copies of our works in any form on the Internet, we would be grateful if you would provide us with the location address or website name. Please contact us at copyright@packt.com with a link to the material.

If you are interested in becoming an author: If there is a topic that you have expertise in and you are interested in either writing or contributing to a book, please visit authors.packtpub.com.

Reviews

Please leave a review. Once you have read and used this book, why not leave a review on the site that you purchased it from? Potential readers can then see and use your unbiased opinion to make purchase decisions, we at Packt can understand what you think about our products, and our authors can see your feedback on their book. Thank you!

For more information about Packt, please visit packt.com.

Getting Started with the NAV Development Environment

1

If you are reading this book, you probably know what Microsoft Dynamics NAV is and want to delve deeper into its customization possibilities. This quick start guide will help you understand different aspects of the NAV development environment, customization of application code, the user interface, and data exchange processes, debugging your code, and designing reports.

The examples in this book are based on Dynamics NAV 2018, but the **Client/server Application Language** (**C/AL**) syntax remains mostly the same since older versions. Recent NAV releases introduced specific language structures designed for interaction with .NET classes and interfaces, as well as task scheduling and handling new UI elements. But these topics are beyond language fundamentals, and hence are not covered in this quick start guide. Code samples accompanying the book can be compiled and run in any version of NAV starting from 2013.

The opening chapter of the book gives an overview of the setup and configuration process, and leads into the integrated development environment. It will cover the following topics:

- Installing the NAV development environment
- Managing NAV server configuration with the **Microsoft Management Console** (**MMC**)
- Managing NAV installation with the NAV Administration Shell
- Introducing the Object Designer
- Exporting and deploying NAV objects

Installing the NAV development environment

Installation of the NAV demo environment is very simple. Running the setup and selecting a predefined configuration is all it takes to install the NAV server with the demonstration database and development tools. On the other hand, experienced users can customize the installation according to their personal needs.

Setup configuration

Installation is started by running `setup.exe` from the root folder of the NAV DVD. After accepting the license agreement, you will be offered two options: either install the predefined demo configuration (install demo), or choose installation options manually (choose an installation option).

If you prefer to run the default installation, all necessary system components will be installed on the same computer. This option will set up NAV Server, NAV Client, the development environment, and a demonstration database with a demo license. This setup will create a new named SQL Server instance, **NAVDEMO**, and restore a database, **Demo Database NAV (11-0)**, on this server instance.

If you select the second option while choosing an installation option, a list of configurations will be suggested. Each of these configurations can be further customized, or installed with the predefined set of components.

Developer configuration is a recommended setup step. Besides the components listed previously, it will also install web server components to provide web access to the NAV server. But you should note that this option requires **Internet Information Services** (**IIS**) running in Windows authentication mode, which is not supported in basic Windows editions. If you are installing NAV on a computer running under Windows 10 Home or Windows 8 Home editions, this option cannot be installed. In this case, disable the **Web Server Components** option manually or choose the **Install Demo** option.

The following screenshot shows the list of components that should be installed. If you choose to disable the optional **Web Server Components**, select the **Not Available** option in the installation menu:

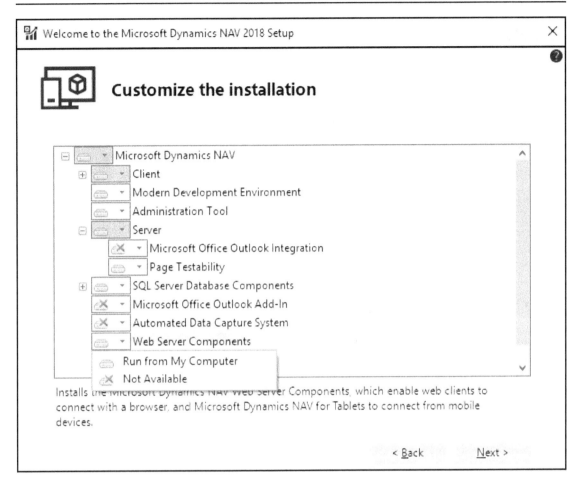

Installation components

Accept all components suggested in this configuration and move to the next step, where you can set up the installation location and other parameters for NAV Server and SQL Server.

Now, if you accept all the default options without changes, the demo database will be created on the default instance of SQL Server (MS SQL Server), if there is one on the computer where the installation is run. If no default instance is found, a new one will be created.

Now you can hit **Apply** and wait until the installation completes.

License information

A demonstration license uploaded with the demo installation supports limited functionality, and most of the examples in this book will not work under the limited demo license. A development license is required to import and run the sample code files, as well as develop your own objects.

To review the license currently uploaded to the server, choose the menu option **Tools** | **License information**. The following line in the license description will tell you that the uploaded license file is intended for demonstration only:

```
Configuration: NAV 2018 Product Demo
```

To upload the developer's license, click **Upload** in the same window and choose the appropriate license file.

Managing NAV server configuration with Microsoft Management Console (MMC)

In the following hands-on example, we will create a copy of the demo database and deploy a new instance of the NAV server connected to the new database. This instance is going to be used as a test server for quality assurance, while the original setup will serve as the development environment. Later in the current chapter, we will see how to move new and modified application objects between databases and servers to make QA (Quality Assurance, or test) and production deployments.

Creating a NAV server instance with MMC

For simplicity, we will run both NAV instances on the same database server. First of all, to prepare another server instance, you need a copy of the demo database. The easiest way to do this is to restore the database from a backup file shipped with the NAV installation DVD. The backup file `Demo Database NAV (11-0).bak` is located under the `SQLDemoDatabase` folder on the DVD. When restoring the database, name it `NAV 110 Test Database`; this name will be used in this chapter.

When the database is restored, we can run MMC and create the service:

1. To start the console, press Windows key + *R* to open the **Run** dialog.
2. In the dialog window, type mmc and press **OK**.
3. Select the **Add or Remove Snap-ins** command from the **File** menu or press *Ctrl + M*.
4. Select **Microsoft Dynamics NAV** from the list of available snap-ins and click **Add**:

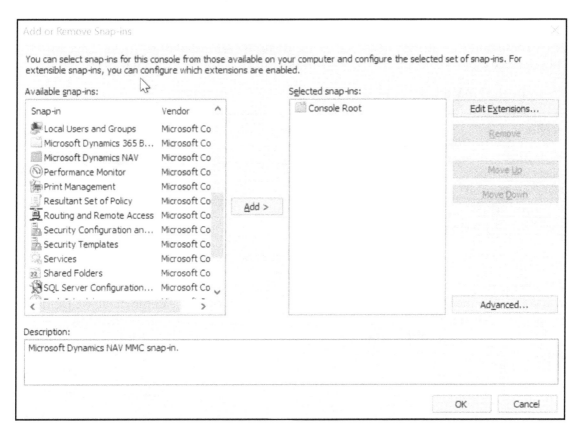

MMC

You will be prompted to enter the name of the NAV server you want to connect to. The default value is **Local**. Leave it unchanged if you are running MMC on the same computer where your NAV Server instance is installed. Otherwise, enter the network name of the server.

The new snap-in will list all instances of the NAV server running on the selected computer. For the brand new demo setup, it shows a single installed server, DynamicsNAV110. Now we want to create another one. Right-click on the snap-in named **Microsoft Dynamics NAV (Local)** in the left pane, under the console root. In the drop-down menu, select the **Add Instance** action. To set up a server instance, you need to specify its name and five numbers for TCP ports used by the service. The default values for ports are 7045 through 7048. These ports are already occupied by the demo server installation, so you have to choose some other numbers. For example, these can be ports 7055 through 7059.

These are the NAV Server TCP ports:

Service	Default port number	Port number for the new server instance
Management services port	7045	7055
Client services port	7046	7056
SOAP services port	7047	7057
Odata services port	7048	7058
Development services port	7049	7059

Enter `NavTestServer` in the **Server Instance** field and confirm instance creation.

All other server configuration options will receive default values. A new server instance will connect to the SQL Server instance NAVDEMO, and open the demo database **Demo Database NAV (11-0)**.

Modifying server settings with MMC

When a new server instance is created, it connects to the default demonstration database, and the database name is what we want to change. To modify the server settings, select the server named **NavTestServer** in the left pane of the management console and click the **Edit** button. Database-related settings are grouped under the **Database** tab. Unfold it and change the value of the **Database Name** field from the default **Demo Database NAV (11-0)** to **NAV 110 Test Database**, then click **Save** to confirm the changes:

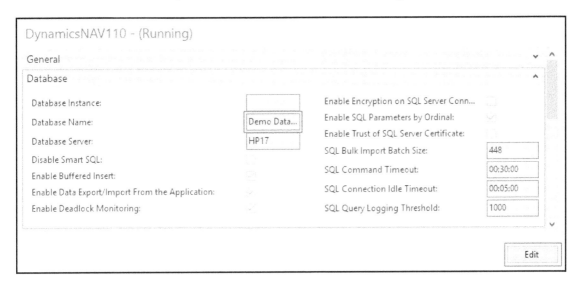

NAV Server instance configuration

When the setup changes are saved, the server must be restarted for the modification to take effect. In order to do so, select the snap-in named **Microsoft Dynamics NAV (Local)** under the console root. The management console will display the list of NAV server instances. Select the **NavTestServer** instance and click **Restart** in the right pane.

Connecting to the new server instance

To connect the **Role Tailored Client** to the test server instantiated in the previous section, start the client and choose the **Select Server** command from the main application menu:

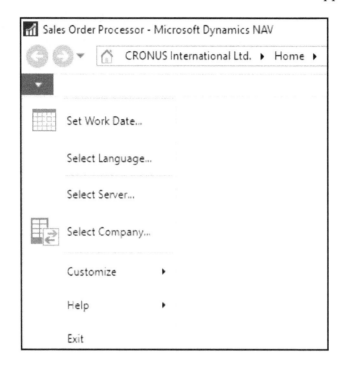

Select Server menu item

In the **ServerAddress** field, type `localhost:7056/NavTestServer` and press *Tab*. Companies that exist in the database will be shown in the **Available Companies** window. The actual list of companies depends on the application version you are using. Local database versions for different countries have different demo companies. Select the company you want to open in the client and confirm the selection.

Managing NAV installation with NAV the Administration Shell

The Dynamics NAV Administration Shell is an alternative to MMC. This is a command-line interface that will be familiar to system administrators. Although the graphical interface is easier and more intuitive, the undoubted benefit of the command-line shell is its ability to combine separate commands into complex batch scripts to automate daily administrative tasks.

Creating a NAV Server instance with Administration Shell

To be able to manage NAV server instances, the Administration Shell must be executed with local administrator credentials. In order to do this, select **Dynamics NAV Administration Shell** in the Windows Start menu, right-click on the application icon, and choose **Run as administrator**. The Administration Shell will list available commands on startup. NAV Administration Shell is actually a PowerShell command window, and each NAV administration command is a PowerShell cmdlet. With PowerShell functionality, you can get the same list of commands with the `Get-Command` cmdlet:

```
Get-Command -Module Microsoft.Dynamics.Nav.Management,
Microsoft.Dynamics.Nav.Apps.Management
```

In the previous section of this chapter, we created a server instance through an MMC snap-in. The same can be done with the `New-NavServerInstance` cmdlet in the NAV Administration Shell:

```
New-NAVServerInstance
 -ManagementServicesPort 7055
 -ClientServicesPort 7056
 -SOAPServicesPort 7057
 -ODataServicesPort 7058
 -DeveloperServicesPort 7059
 -DatabaseServer localhost
 -DatabaseInstance NAVDEMO
 -DatabaseName "NAV 110 Test Database"
 -ServerInstance NavTestServer
 -ClientServicesCredentialType Windows
```

Note that we provide all parameters, including TCP ports and the database name. Unlike the GUI approach, there is no need to modify server settings after creating an instance.

Managing the NAV server with the Administration Shell

Now the brand new service must be started. To start it, run the following command in the Administration Shell:

```
Start-NAVServerInstance -ServerInstance NavTestServer
```

The same can be done with a Windows system cmdlet, `Start-Service`:

```
Start-Service -Name 'MicrosoftDynamicsNavServer$NavTestServer'
```

Note that, in this case, we must provide the full-service name, which includes a prefix, `MicrosoftDynamicsNavServer$`. When we operate with cmdlets developed specifically for NAV Administration Shell, we only provide the NAV server instance name to the command. The actual server name always begins with the same string, which is implicitly added to the parameter by NAV cmdlets. Keep this in mind when you develop your own Powershell code and pass service names between NAV and system cmdlets.

When you no longer need the additional server instance, delete it with the `Remove-NAVServerInstance` cmdlet:

```
Remove-NAVServerInstance -ServerInstance NavTestServer
```

There are some other cmdlets available in the NAV Administration Shell that can simplify your daily administration activities.

If you are already familiar with Windows Powershell, you probably know about a very powerful cmdlet, `Get-WmiObject`, that can retrieve information about available **Windows Management Instrumentation** (**WMI**) classes. For example, with `Get-WmiObject`, you can list all installed NAV services:

```
Get-WmiObject -Class Win32_Service | Where-Object {$_.Name -imatch "DynamicsNAV"}
```

Services will be listed, along with their state and some other properties.

The NAV Administration Shell provides a shortcut for this command. `Get-NAVServerInstance` will yield the same result, displaying a list of available NAV services.

With the PowerShell pipeline, the resulting list can be filtered. For example, here is the command to select only running services:

```
Get-WmiObject -Class Win32_Service | Where-Object {$_.Name -imatch
"DynamicsNAV" -and $_.State -eq "Running"}
```

Or this is the same without the explicit call to `Get-WmiObject`:

```
Get-NAVServerInstance | Where-Object {$_.State -eq "Running"}
```

Now the result set returned by the previous cmdlet can be sent to the pipeline to stop all running services:

```
Get-WmiObject -Class Win32_Service |
  Where-Object {$_.Name -imatch "DynamicsNAV" -and $_.State -eq "Running"}
| Stop-Service
```

Now start all stopped services:

```
Get-WmiObject -Class Win32_Service |
  Where-Object {$_.Name -imatch "DynamicsNAV" -and $_.State -eq "Running"}
| Start-Service
```

Then restart all running NAV services:

```
Get-WmiObject -Class Win32_Service |
  Where-Object {$_.Name -imatch "DynamicsNAV" -and $_.State -eq "Running"}
| Restart-Service
```

Introducing the Object Designer

NAV presents its development capabilities through its own integrated development environment: **Client/Server Integrated Development Environment (C/SIDE)**.

C/SIDE and application objects

The Dynamics NAV Development Environment is accessed from the Windows Start menu. If you just installed Microsoft Dynamics NAV, the development environment will open the database that was specified during installation. If for some reason the database does not open automatically, choose the **Database | Open** option from the **File** menu. This will invoke the open **Database** dialog, where you can specify the name of your development server and the database.

The first thing you see after starting the development environment is the **Object Designer**. On first start, the development environment connects to the database specified during the installation. If this does not happen, and all you see is a blank window, choose **File** | **Database** | **Open** from the main menu and select the SQL Server and the database name where the development database was created:

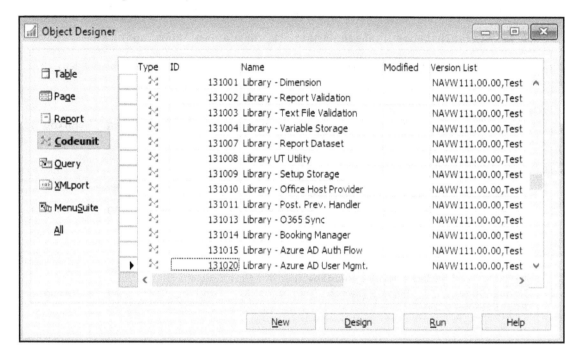

Object Designer interface

Although these application elements are called objects, they should not be confused with objects in object-oriented programming. C/SIDE does not actually support OOP. Developers can create new objects of existing types, but cannot create new object types or classes.

The following table gives an overview of NAV object types and their functions:

Object	Description
Table	NAV table objects are mapped to SQL Server tables and used to access database data. Tables provide interfaces to read and manipulate data. Table objects are covered in detail in Chapter 3, *Tables - Creating Data Structure*.
Page	The primary method of presenting data to the user is to show it on a page. Nearly everything you see in the client interface is a page. Chapter 4, *Designing User Interface*, covers the development of the user interface, and pages in particular.
Report	Use reports to add reporting capabilities to your application and present user data in a structured way. Read more about reports in Chapter 7, *Presenting Data in Reports*.
Codeunit	A codeunit can be considered as a collection of functions of code that can be used by other objects. This is the equivalent of a library in many other languages. Almost all C/SIDE objects can contain program code, but codeunits are designed solely for this purpose. codeunits are explained in Chapter 2, *Codeunits - Structuring C/AL Code*.
Query	C/SIDE provides developers with a toolbox for designing database queries without the need to write SQL code. Queries help improve the performance of the application when it comes to joining tables to select related records from different sources. Queries are not covered in this book.
XMLport	XMLports provide a simple interface for configuring hierarchical data structures in XML format for data exchange. They supply a quick method of exporting and importing data with the minimum amount of programming. More on XMLports in Chapter 5, *Exchanging Data with XML Ports*.
MenuSuite	Links to application areas, pages, and reports are presented in the user interface in a structured user menu through a set of MenuSuite objects. You will design your own user menu in Chapter 4, *Designing User Interface*.

All objects are identified by the object type, ID, and name. A sample object created in the next section demonstrates how to create an application object and assign a name and ID to it.

Hello World example

To demonstrate how to design objects in C/SIDE, we will follow a traditional example and write a simple `Hello World` application. In Dynamics NAV, this is going to be a line of code in the `OnRun` trigger of a codeunit. To create a codeunit, switch to the codeunits list in the **Object Designer** window. Click *Alt + C*, or choose the codeunit icon in the left pane, to select codeunits. To create a new object, press *Ctrl + N* (or choose **File | New action** in the main application menu).

 A developer license is required to create new objects or design existing application objects. To change the license, run the menu action **Tools | License Information**, then import the license with the **Upload** button.

The `MESSAGE` function is used to display a UI message; we will use it to display the greeting. The `OnRun` trigger is automatically added to the object by the editor, so the only thing to do now is to write a code line that shows the message:

```
OnRun()
MESSAGE('Hello World');
```

Now, save the object (**File | Save**). The new object does not have a name and ID yet, so the first time it is saved, you will be prompted to name the codeunit. Enter `50500` as the ID and `Hello World` for the codeunit name.

The object name is a string, up to 30 characters long, that should describe the object's function to the developer. It must be unique for each object type. ID is a positive integer number used internally by the system. A NAV developer license allows you to create objects with IDs ranging from 50000 to 50999, and all objects described in this book will receive IDs starting from `50500`:

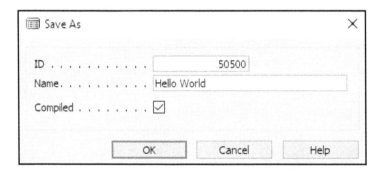

Save As dialog window

---

[20]

Apart from two fields identifying the object, the dialog contains a **Compiled** flag that specifies whether the object should be compiled before saving. An uncompiled object cannot be executed, so leave the flag checked and click **OK**.

Running objects from the Object Designer

To execute the new codeunit, select it in the **Object Designer** and click the **Run** button located under the list of objects. This action will start the role-tailored client and execute the object code displaying the **Hello World** message box.

This method of executing object code is not intended to be employed by users to perform their daily tasks. Normally, objects are invoked from a user menu (we will learn how to do this in one of the following chapters). But it is very useful for debugging and testing purposes to quickly run an object during development. Any object, except MenuSuites, can be executed this way.

Exporting and deploying NAV objects

To exchange objects between different databases, it is possible to export them in an external file and import it into a new destination. NAV supports two file formats for application objects: .txt and .fob. The former is object source code in plain text format, while .fob is a native NAV format containing compiled code. Since objects in the .fob file are already in the compiled state, they don't have to be recompiled after import in order to be executed. Objects imported from text files must be compiled first; otherwise, they cannot be run.

Another significant difference between the two object formats is the license permission required to work with files. To be able to export and import plain text files, you need a developer's license, which allows you to create and edit specific objects being processed. The .fob file format does not impose such restrictions on the file exchange process. This is the reason why .fob files are typically used to export new or modified objects from a development/test environment and deploy them to a production server. Usually, the production server is run under an end user license without development access to application code, and there is no possibility to import plain text files.

Besides, software developers usually don't want to disclose source code when selling their solutions. The native .fob format hides the application source behind compiled bytecode, which is impossible with .txt files.

In the **Object Designer** window, select the **50500** codeunit you created earlier and choose the menu option **File | Export**, then select the file location. In the **File Type** field, choose ***.txt** as the file format, and press the **Save** button. This will create a file containing the source code for the codeunit:

```
OBJECT Codeunit 50500 Hello World
{
    OBJECT-PROPERTIES
    {
        Date=14.08.18;
        Time=16:39:41;
        Modified=Yes;
        Version List=PACKT QSG;
    }
    PROPERTIES
    {
        OnRun=BEGIN
                 MESSAGE('Hello World');
              END;
    }
    CODE
    {
        BEGIN
        END.
    }
}
```

To import the object into another database, open a copy of the demo database and invoke the **File | Import** command from the main menu. Select the exported file and click **Open**.

If an object being imported from a text file already exists in the database, the new version will replace the old one without a confirmation request. Be careful and double-check that the database object can be safely deleted.

Managing objects with the Dynamics NAV Development Shell

Similar to the NAV 2018 Administration Shell, the NAV 2018 Development Shell provides access to PowerShell cmdlets for the management of application objects. Development tasks, such as object export, import, and compilation, can be automated with the Development Shell. The same as Administration Shell, NAV Development Shell can be run from the Start menu. On startup, it imports several modules. We will now take a closer look at one of them: `Microsoft.Dynamics.Nav.Model.Tools`.

To list all cmdlets available in the `Microsoft.Dynamics.Nav.Model.Tools` module, run this:

```
Get-Command -Module Microsoft.Dynamics.Nav.Model.Tools
```

As an alternative to the method described previously, the import/export procedure can be performed in the NAV Development Shell. To do it, run the following commands one by one.

The first cmdlet will export objects defined by the `Filter` parameter from the specified NAV server to the disk:

```
Export-NAVApplicationObject -DatabaseName "Demo Database NAV (11-0)"
    -DatabaseServer "localhost\NAVDEMO" -Path "C:\NAV Objects\COD50500.txt"
    -Filter "Type=Codeunit;ID=50500"
```

Typically, you apply a `Filter` based on the object type and name, but other object properties can be used for filtering as well. For example, you may want to export all modified objects:

```
Export-NAVApplicationObject -DatabaseName "Demo Database NAV (11-0)"
  -DatabaseServer "localhost\NAVDEMO"
    -Path "C:\NAV Objects\Modified.txt" -Filter "Modified=Yes"
```

Or export all object labeled with the version `PACKT`:

```
Export-NAVApplicationObject -DatabaseName "Demo Database NAV (11-0)"
    -DatabaseServer "localhost\NAVDEMO"
    -Path "C:\NAV Objects\COD50500.txt" -Filter "Version List=*PACKT*"
```

To import the objects, run the **Import-NAVApplicationObject** cmdlet:

```
Import-NAVApplicationObject -Path "C:\NAV Objects\COD50500.txt"
    -DatabaseName "Demo Database NAV (11-0)" -DatabaseServer
"localhost\NAVDEMO"
```

Imported objects must be compiled in the new database:

```
Compile-NAVApplicationObject -DatabaseName "Demo Database NAV (11-0)"
    -DatabaseServer "localhost\NAVDEMO" -NavServerName DynamicsNAV110
    -Filter "Type=Codeunit;ID=50500"
```

You can compile all objects in the database, or use the Filter parameter to select a subset.

Now, let's combine all these code samples into one Powershell function that can export, import, and compile the object with a single command. To do this, we will need the PowerShell IDE, which can be started from the Windows Applications menu. The application name is **powershell_ide**. Place the following code in the PowerShell editor and run it:

```
if ([Environment]::Is64BitProcess)
{
    $RtcFolder =
        'HKLM:\SOFTWARE\Wow6432Node\Microsoft\Microsoft Dynamics
NAV\110\RoleTailored Client'
}
else
{
    $RtcFolder = 'HKLM:\SOFTWARE\Microsoft\Microsoft Dynamics
NAV\110\RoleTailored Client'
}

Test-Path $RtcFolder
$IdeModulePath = (Join-Path (Get-ItemProperty $RtcFolder).Path
Microsoft.Dynamics.Nav.Ide.psm1)
Import-Module $IdeModulePath

function Deploy-ObjectsToTestServer
{
    Param(
        [Parameter(Mandatory = $true)]
        [string] $DevelopmentDatabaseName,
        [Parameter(Mandatory = $true)]
        [string] $TestDatabaseName,
        [Parameter(Mandatory = $true)]
        [string] $DevelopmentServerName,
        [Parameter(Mandatory = $false, ParameterSetName =
        "SeparateTestServer")]
```

```
        [string] $TestServerName,
        [Parameter(Mandatory = $false, ParameterSetName =
        "SingelServerSetup")]
        [switch] $SingleServer = $true,
        [Parameter(Mandatory = $true)]
        [string] $NavServerInstance,
        [Parameter(Mandatory = $true)]
        [string] $ObjectFilter
    )

    if ($SingleServer)
    {
        $TestServerName = $DevelopmentServerName
    }

    [string] $tempFileName = [System.IO.Path]::GetTempFileName() +
    ".txt"

    Export-NAVApplicationObject
        -DatabaseName $DevelopmentDatabaseName -DatabaseServer
        $DevelopmentServerName
        -Path $tempFileName -Filter $ObjectFilter
    Import-NAVApplicationObject
        -Path $tempFileName -DatabaseName $TestDatabaseName -
        DatabaseServer $TestServerName
    Compile-NAVApplicationObject
        -DatabaseName $TestDatabaseName -DatabaseServer $TestServerName
        -NavServerName $NavServerInstance -Filter $ObjectFilter
}
```

Now you can easily prepare your modification for testing with a single command:

```
Deploy-ObjectsToTestServer -DevelopmentDatabaseName "Demo Database NAV
(11-0)" -TestDatabaseName "NAV 110 Test Database" -DevelopmentServerName
localhost\NAVDEMO -SingleServer -NavServerInstance "NavTestServer" -
ObjectFilter "ID=50500..50599"
```

This command will export all objects with IDs from 50500 to 50599 from the development database, Demo Database NAV (11-0), into a temporary file, import it into the NAV 110 Test Database, and compile all imported objects.

Summary

The first chapter introduced the development environment and the basic object model of Microsoft Dynamics NAV. We installed and configured development tools and instantiated an additional server instance for testing purposes. We learned to create and configure server instances in different ways: with MMC or NAV Administration Shell.

The chapter also gave an overview of other capabilities of the NAV PowerShell harness. Besides administering server instances, it gives access to development tools to automate development activities, such as exchanging objects between databases and compiling them.

Also, we started writing simple C/AL code—a topic that will continue in the next chapter. We will write more advanced codeunits and get familiar with the structure of a codeunit. The second chapter will demonstrate the capabilities of C/AL for accessing the database and manipulating data.

Codeunits - Structuring C/AL Code

2

The first chapter of this book briefly introduced C/SIDE objects and the basic concept of the object model. We created a simple codeunit that simply shows a text message when executed. This chapter gives a deeper overview of the C/AL language and its capabilities. To introduce the internal NAV programming language, the chapter presents the concept of a codeunit—a container of code that is called by other objects, a code library. The first chapter already gave a short foreword on codeunits; now we will continue with the following topics:

- Compiling a codeunit and error handling
- Declaring and calling functions
- Function parameters and return values
- Declaring variables—variable scope
- Passing variables by value and by reference
- Record variables
- codeunit variables—calling functions from other codeunits
- Text constants

Compiling a codeunit and error handling

As we already know, codeunits, as well as other application objects, are created in the Object Designer. The first time you save a new object, you will be requested to assign an ID number and a name to it and compile the object. But the **Compiled** option prevents saving the object if its code has syntax errors. Let's see how we can handle the commonplace situation of saving an object before fixing bugs.

Handling compilation errors

If the code of an object contains a syntax error, an attempt to compile this object will fail, and the compilation will stop on the first encountered error. Let's modify the `Hello World` example from the previous chapter and see how the Object Designer treats compilation errors. Suppose we have forgotten to put the apostrophe at the end of the text line, leaving the constant unterminated. This is a syntax error that prevents compilation:

```
OnRun()
    MESSAGE('Hello World);
```

Now, try to save the object with the **Compiled** option checked. The Object Designer will display an error message notifying you that there is a syntax error in the code and underlining the erroneous code block, as follows:

Syntax error highlighting

Underlining and cursor positioning help the developer identify the particular block of code containing the error.

 An object containing erroneous code that cannot be compiled is not saved when the **Save** dialog is called with the **Compiled** option. Changes are saved to the database only after the object is successfully compiled.

Although an object with a syntax error cannot be saved in a compiled state, it is still possible to save changes without compilation before starting to look for errors. To do so, invoke the **Save** dialog (press *Ctrl + S* or select the **File | Save** menu command) and uncheck the **Compiled** checkbox. Now the object cannot be executed, but you can carefully inspect the code without the risk of losing your modifications.

One of the specific features of the C/SIDE development environment is how the compiler reports syntax errors. All compilation errors are stated one by one. If the object being compiled has more than one error, there is no way to see them all in a list. You must fix the first error the compiler stops on to move on and find another one.

Declaring and calling functions

When you open a NAV application object in the designer and review its code, function names are probably among the first things you notice. Code is structured in blocks with function headers clearly highlighted in bold font. But if you try to change a function's declaration—for example, change its name or add a parameter—you will see that the line with the function declaration is not editable.

Function names, return types, and parameter lists are accessed through a separate editor, and cannot be modified in the main code editor window.

In the next example, we will create a simple function to illustrate the process of declaring C/AL functions. This is a slightly modified version of the previous `Hello World` example. Now, we will not show the message in the standard codeunit trigger, but delegate the greeting to a local function instead.

In the **Object Designer** window, create a new codeunit. Save the new object as codeunit **50505 Simple Function Example**.

While in the code editor, choose the **View | C/AL Globals** option from the main menu, or alternatively click *Ctrl + G*. This action opens a **C/AL Globals** window where global variables, text constants, and functions are declared. We will cover variables and text constants later in this chapter; for now, open the **Functions** tab and write the function name as `SayHello`:

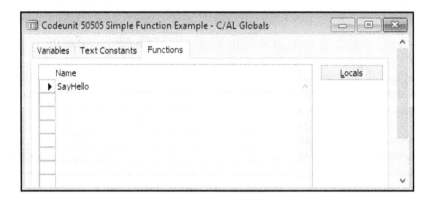

Function declaration

Close the window to return to the code editor window—you will see the new function, `SayHello`. Move the cursor to a line below the function header and write its code, then invoke the function from the `OnRun` trigger, as shown in the code snippet that follows:

```
OnRun()
    SayHello;

LOCAL SayHello()
    MESSAGE('Hello World');
```

As with previous examples, save the object and compile it, then close the code editor and press **Run** to execute the codeunit and see the text message.

Function parameters and return values

In the previous example, we simply call a function that displays a hardcoded message. But if we want to make the function more flexible and able to show different text, we must pass a text parameter into the function. Function parameters in NAV are declared in the same way as functions themselves. A line of code representing the function declaration in the code editor is not editable. Parameters are described in a separate editor window instead. In this section, we will see how to pass parameters to a function and return a resulting value from it.

How to add parameters to a function

Let's modify the codeunit so that the message to be shown to the user will be passed in the function call instead of hardcoding it in the function body itself. From the previous section, you already know how to access the list of functions. Now, there is only one function we named SayHello. Change its name to ShowMessage and close the C/AL Global window to return to the code editor.

Now, let's add a text parameter to the ShowMessage function. To access the list of function parameters, position the cursor in any line inside the function and choose the **View |
Locals** menu option, or click *Ctrl + L*. This action opens a **C/AL Locals** window that contains local declarations for the function. In the **Name** field of the table, enter a parameter named **MessageText** and choose its type in the drop-down list in the **DataType** field. This parameter should be of type **Text**. The other fields of the table are left blank.
The **Subtype** property is not applicable to text variables, and the blank value of **Length** means that the length of the text string in unlimited:

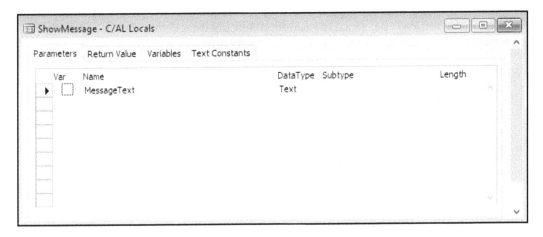

Function parameter declaration

Now, just close the window, and you are good to go; a text parameter can be passed to the function. Note that the function header was also updated. You can see function's parameter in the text editor, although you cannot modify it. Modify the OnRun and ShowMessage functions as follows:

```
OnRun()
    ShowMessage('Just another text message!');

LOCAL ShowMessage(MessageText : Text)
    MESSAGE(MessageText);
```

Function return value

Now, let's see how to return a value from a function to the calling code. The next example continues depicting the topic of function parameters. This time, we will create a function that accepts three parameters and returns the minimum of the three input values.

Create a new codeunit and declare a function in it. Call it Min. After inserting the function, return to the code editor, position the cursor on an empty line under the function name, and access the **C/AL Locals** window. In the **Parameters** tab, insert the parameter named A and choose **Integer** in the **DataType** field. When done, move to the next line and declare the **Integer** parameter B, then C. If you close C/AL Locals now, function Min with three Integer parameters will show in the editor as follows:

```
LOCAL Min(A : Integer;B : Integer;C : Integer)
```

Now, it does not return any value. To assign a return type to the function, open the **C/AL Locals** window if you already closed it and activate the **Return Value** tab. The function value can be described with three properties: **Name**, **Return Type**, and **Length**. Right now, all we need is the return type. Since the function accepts integer parameters and returns one of these as the result, select the **Integer** type in the **Return Type** field.

The source code of the function Min is as follows:

```
LOCAL PROCEDURE Min(A : Integer;B : Integer;C : Integer) : Integer;
  IF A <= B THEN BEGIN
    IF A <= C THEN
      EXIT(A);
  END ELSE
    IF B <= C THEN
      EXIT(B);

  EXIT(C);
```

To return a value to the caller, we use the EXIT statement. Depending on the results of the comparison operation function, Min will return one of the values A, B, or C. If the function completes execution without calling EXIT, zero or an empty value will be returned implicitly. Integer-typed function will yield 0 in this case.

Although it is not mandatory to return a value from a function explicitly, it is highly recommended to use EXIT. Explicit returns improve code readability.

Besides the function return type and the EXIT keyword, this example introduces conditional statements in C/AL.

To test the function, call it from the OnRun trigger of the codeunit:

```
MESSAGE(STRSUBSTNO('Minimum of three values is %1',Min(123,22,60)));
```

Since our Min function returns a numeric value, and MESSAGE accepts a text string, we cannot pass the function return value directly— the integer must be converted to text first. The most common way of doing such a conversion is the STRSUBSTNO function. It is especially handy when you need to construct a text string that includes variable components defined at runtime. STRSUBSTNO accepts a variable number of parameters, the first being a text string with placeholders—numbers preceded by the % symbol: %1, %2, %3, and so on, up to 10 values. When the function is executed, placeholders are replaced with function arguments following the text expression.

Declaring variables – variable scope

As we saw in the previous topic in this chapter, functions and function parameters in C/SIDE are not declared directly in the code editor. Instead, they are entered in a tabular view presented in a separate editor. This is also true for variables; we do not describe variables in C/AL code, but access the variable declaration through the C/AL Locals and **C/AL Globals** windows.

Local variables

To illustrate the declaration and use of local variables, we will implement a simple algorithm comparing two strings to find the editorial distance, or Levenshtein distance. This distance is a measure of similarity between strings that is often used in various text processing systems to suggest automatic correction for typos.

The RecursiveDistance function in this example implements a recursive version of the algorithm. Following the description of function parameters in the previous section, you can declare the function, assign a return type to it, and insert four parameters, so that the declaration looks as follows:

```
LOCAL RecursiveDistance(S1 : Text;S2 : Text;Position1 : Integer;Position2 :
Integer) : Integer
```

Now, the function requires a single local variable that is declared in the same window, C/AL Locals, as function parameters. To add a local variable, position input focus under the function name and open C/AL Locals, then activate the **Variables** tab and insert a line in the table. Enter **Dist** in the **Name** field, and choose **Integer** in the **DataType** drop-down list.

Close the variable declaration window. Now you can use the `Dist` variable in your code, although unlike function parameters, it is not shown anywhere in the code editor. To view the list of function variables, you have to open C/AL Locals again.

Now, let's write the code of the function itself. The first thing we do is define the base case, shown as follows, which does require recursive calls:

```
LOCAL RecursiveDistance(S1 : Text;S2 : Text;Position1 : Integer;Position2 :
Integer) : Integer
IF Position1 = 0 THEN
  EXIT(Position2);
IF Position2 = 0 THEN
  EXIT(Position1);

IF S1[Position1] = S2[Position2] THEN
  Dist := 0
ELSE
  Dist := 1;

EXIT(
  Min(
    RecursiveDistance(S1,S2,Position1 - 1,Position2) + 1,
    RecursiveDistance(S1,S2,Position1,Position2 - 1) + 1,
    RecursiveDistance(S1,S2,Position1 - 1,Position2 - 1) + Dist));
```

In the previous code, the local `Dist` variable indicates whether there is a difference between strings in the current position. It assumes a 0 value if symbols are equal, and 1 otherwise. Since `Dist` is a local variable, a new copy of the variable will be created in each call of the `RecursiveDistance` function.

The `Min` function called from `RecursiveDistance` is the one described in the previous section.

Variable properties – declaring arrays

The following example implements a simple algorithm, finding the longest common substring of two given strings.

Start writing the code for creating the `FindLongestCommonSubstring` function, then change its return type and add two text parameters:

```
LOCAL PROCEDURE FindLongestCommonSubstring(S1 : Text[100];S2 : Text[100])
Substring : Text;
```

The text variables `S1` and `S2` in the function declaration have limited lengths; they are declared as `Text[100]`. The length of a text variable is specified in the Length column in the variable declaration window.

Note the literal `Substring` in the function declaration line. This is a named return value. So far, we have assigned return types to functions and used the `EXIT` statement to return the function execution result. An alternative way is to give it a name and use it as a local variable. `EXIT` is not required in this case; the last value assigned to the `Substring` will be returned to the calling code.

The next step is to declare local variables that will be used in the function. We will apply the dynamic programming approach to the problem, which means that intermediate calculation results must be stored in memory, and we will need a data structure for storage. This data structure is a two-dimensional array of integer numbers, which are the calculated lengths of all substring matches.

To declare an array, open C/AL Locals, switch to **Variables**, and add an **Integer** variable, **Length**. So far, it is no different from declaring a scalar variable. Now, expand the **View** menu group in the application menu and select the **Properties** command. Or alternatively, press *Shift + F4*. This command opens variable properties, which include **ID** and **Dimensions**. For other variable types, the list of properties may differ, but so far, we are interested only in the **Dimensions** property.

The property ID is the unique number identifying the variable. It is required for the compiler in its internal representation of the object. The ID is automatically assigned by C/SIDE and never used in the application code. Usually, there is no need to change it.

By default, the **Dimensions** property has a value, **<Undefined>**, which means that we are dealing with a scalar integer. To turn it into an array, enter the array length in the **Dimensions** field. For a linear or one-dimensional array, this is a single number, representing the number of elements in the array. To declare a two-dimensional array, we specify the number of rows and columns, separating them with a semicolon: `100;100`.

Set up the dimensions for the array variable, close the variable properties window, and declare the remaining local variables as follows:

```
Length : ARRAY [100,100] OF Integer;
Longest : Integer;
I : Integer;
J : Integer;
```

And the following is the code of the function itself. Addressing an element of a one-dimensional array is no different from addressing a symbol in a string (since a string is basically an array of symbols); we just refer to it by a number in square brackets. For example, S[1] means the first element of the S array. For multidimensional arrays, an element is identified by a number in each dimension, and these numbers are specified in square brackets divided by a comma: Length[5,8] is an element in the fifth row and eighth column of the two-dimensional array:

```
LOCAL PROCEDURE FindLongestCommonSubstring(S1 : Text[100];S2 :
Text[100]) Substring : Text;
  FOR I := 1 TO STRLEN(S1) DO
    FOR J := 1 TO STRLEN(S2) DO
      IF S1[I] = S2[J] THEN BEGIN
        IF (I = 1) OR (J = 1) THEN
          Length[I,J] := 1
        ELSE
          Length[I,J] := Length[I - 1,J - 1] + 1;

        IF Length[I,J] > Longest THEN BEGIN
          Longest := Length[I,J];
          Substring := COPYSTR(S1,I - Longest + 1,Longest);
        END ELSE
          IF Length[I,J] = Longest THEN
            Substring := Substring + COPYSTR(S1,I - Longest +
            1,Longest);
      END ELSE
        Length[I,J] := 0;
```

To test the result, call the `FindLongestCommonSubstring` function in the codeunit's `OnRun` trigger, as we do in other examples:

```
OnRun()
  MESSAGE(FindLongestCommonSubstring('collaboration','laboratory'));
```

This message will tell us that the two words `collaboration` and `laboratory` have a common part, `laborat`.

Global variables

A global variable is available throughout the object where it is declared, but is not visible to other objects. Global variables are declared in the **C/AL Globals** window. This window is already familiar to us, since functions are declared through the same interface. Global variables are accessed in the **Variables** tab.

To demonstrate the use of global variables, we will modify one of the previous examples and rewrite the function, calculating the edit distance. The function will be altered to use global variables instead of passing strings as parameters. For this example, we will need two global variables. Create a new codeunit and declare these two variables:

```
GlobalString1 : Text;
GlobalString2 : Text;
```

Now, let's see how the body of the function will change, considering that we don't have a local copy of the two strings in each function call, but use global instances instead. In the same codeunit, shown here, write the modified functions `Distance` and `RecursiveDistance`:

```
OnRun()
    MESSAGE(FORMAT(Distance('string','wrong')));

LOCAL Distance(S1 : Text;S2 : Text) : Integer
    GlobalString1 := UPPERCASE(S1);
    GlobalString2 := UPPERCASE(S2);
    EXIT(RecursiveDistance(STRLEN(S1),STRLEN(S2)));

LOCAL RecursiveDistance(Position1 : Integer;Position2 : Integer) : Integer
    IF Position1 = 0 THEN
        EXIT(Position2);
    IF Position2 = 0 THEN
        EXIT(Position1);

    IF GlobalString1[Position1] = GlobalString2[Position2] THEN
        Dist := 0
    ELSE
        Dist := 1;

    EXIT(
        Min(
            RecursiveDistance(Position1 - 1,Position2) + 1,
            RecursiveDistance(Position1,Position2 - 1) + 1,
            RecursiveDistance(Position1 - 1,Position2 - 1) + Dist));
```

The `Min` function in this example is the same function that was described in the *Function return value* section, and can simply be copied from that section.

First of all, the `Distance` function does not pass its two parameters down to `RecuriveDistance`, but initializes the global variables `GlobalString1` and `GlobalString2`. The same applies to `RecuriveDistance` itself. A clear benefit of this refactoring of the code is that unlike the first version, the restructured function does not create copies of two strings in each recursive call. This makes the algorithm less demanding in terms of memory.

Passing variables by value and by reference

To simplify the example, we will skip the sorting of the input array, but instead generate a random array whose elements are already sorted in ascending order.
The `GenerateRandomSortedArray` function will do this: it simply fills an array with random values, each value greater than the previous one. A generated array is the result that must be returned from the function. But the function return value can only be a scalar; it is not possible to return an array directly as a function value. A `ByVar` parameter can help us to work around this problem. If we pass an array variable to `GenerateRandomSortedArray` by reference, any changes made inside the function will be visible to the calling code. Let's see how this works.

Inside the function, declare an `InputArray` parameter of type `Integer` and set the checkmark in the `Var` field. To complete the declaration of the array, open the properties of the variable and change the value of the **Dimensions** property to **100**:

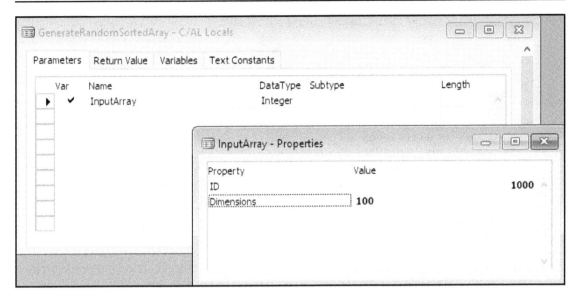

Declaring a ByVar parameter

Besides the `InputArray` parameter, the function also has one local variable:

```
I : Integer;
```

The following is the code that generated a pseudo-sorted array. It just fills the array with random values, with each value greater than the previous one:

```
LOCAL PROCEDURE GenerateRandomSortedAray(VAR InputArray : ARRAY [100] OF
Integer)
  InputArray[1] := RANDOM(100);
  FOR I := 2 TO ARRAYLEN(InputArray) DO
    InputArray[I] := InputArray[I - 1] + RANDOM(10);
```

Now, when the sorted array is prepared, let's look at the search function. The function is called `BinarySearch` and has three local variables:

```
LeftIndex : Integer;
RightIndex : Integer;
MidIndex : Integer;
```

As you can see in the following code, the array parameter in the search function is also passed by reference:

```
LOCAL BinarySearch(VAR InputArray : ARRAY [100] OF Integer;SearchValue :
Integer) : Integer
  LeftIndex := 1;
```

```
RightIndex := ARRAYLEN(InputArray);

WHILE LeftIndex < RightIndex DO BEGIN
  IF InputArray[LeftIndex] = SearchValue THEN
    EXIT(LeftIndex);
  IF InputArray[RightIndex] = SearchValue THEN
    EXIT(RightIndex);

  MidIndex := (LeftIndex + RightIndex) DIV 2;
  IF InputArray[MidIndex] < SearchValue THEN
    LeftIndex := MidIndex
  ELSE
    RightIndex := MidIndex;
END;

EXIT(0);
```

And finally, we bind the two functions together in the `OnRun` trigger. The `IntArray` array is declared as a local variable in the trigger to be passed to both functions, `GenerateRandomSortedAray` and `BinarySearch`:

```
IntArray : ARRAY [100] OF Integer;
Index : Integer;
```

The `Index` variable keeps the position of the element we seek in the array. If it's not found, 0 is returned:

```
OnRun()
  GenerateRandomSortedArray(IntArray);
  Index := BinarySearch(IntArray,IntArray[50]);
  IF Index = 0 THEN
    MESSAGE(ValueNotFoundMsg)
  ELSE
    MESSAGE(FoundValueMsg,Index,25);
```

Two text constants used in this code sample should be declared in **C/AL Globals** as follows:

Name	ConstValue
ValueNotFoundMsg	Value not found in array
FoundValueMsg	Element number %1 has the value %2

The message either shows the position in which the element was found, or informs the user that it is not present in the array.

Record variables

Record is one of the most important and widely used data types in C/AL code. A Record variable refers to a database table, and allows us to retrieve and manipulate table data. A code example in this section will demonstrate how to search data with a Record variable and update found records. This is a more business-related scenario than those we coded in previous sections. As an example, we will update sales prices for an item based on certain criteria calculated from other database tables.

Iterating over a recordset

To declare a Record variable, you must enter its name, select the **Record** data type in the **DataType** field, and choose one of the database tables as the variable's **Subtype**. In the next code sample, we will read data from a Item table, which must be declared as a variable. In a new codeunit, create a function, **UpdatePrices**, and add a local variable as shown in the screenshot:

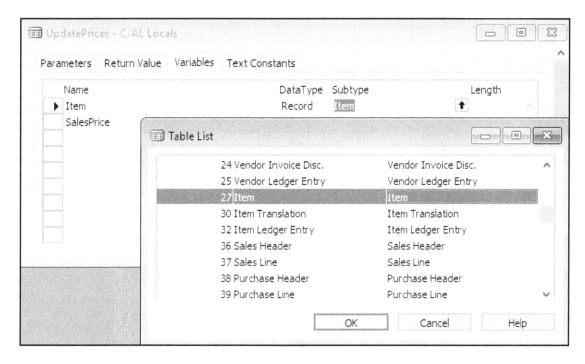

Declaring a Record variable

Then add another variable, so that there are two local variables in the function:

```
Item : Record Item;
SalesPrice : Decimal;
```

The UpdatePrices function will loop through all items, looking for sales in the past month. If there are none, the last sales price will be reduced by 10%. Each of these logical operations—searching for sales prices in the given period, identifying the last price, and updating the item price—are implemented in separate functions and demonstrate different aspects of data manipulation in C/AL. Now we will go step by step through all these functions:

```
LOCAL PROCEDURE UpdatePrices();
  IF Item.FINDSET THEN
    REPEAT
      IF NOT SalesInPastMonthExist(Item."No.") THEN BEGIN
        SalesPrice := FindLastSalesInvoicePrice(Item."No.");
        IF SalesPrice = 0 THEN
          SalesPrice := Item."Unit Price";
        IF SalesPrice > 0 THEN
          SetSalesLineDiscountForItem(Item."No.",SalesPrice *
          0.9,WORKDATE + 1,CALCDATE('<+1M>',WORKDATE));
      END;
    UNTIL Item.NEXT = 0;
```

This code snippet presents the FINDSET function—one of the C/AL functions for searching records in a tables. FINDSET retrieves a recordset from the table and transfers data from the first found record into the Record variable. So, after calling Item.FINDSET, the Item variable will be initialized with values from the first record in the Item table. All other records are buffered and can be iterated through with a loop. A typical pattern of processing a recordset is to read it from the database with the FINDSET function and use a REPEAT.UNTIL loop to traverse all records in the recordset. The NEXT function moves the position of the record pointer to the next record in the dataset.

 FINDSET returns a Boolean value indicating whether any records were found. If no records were retrieved and the return value is not handled by the C/AL code, a runtime error occurs.

Filtering records

The previous example that iterated over the items listed all records in the Item table. If we don't need to retrieve all records from a table, but want to restrict the dataset to some specific records, we apply filters to the record. Two system functions exist for this purpose in C/AL: SETRANGE and SETFILTER. Let's take a look at an example of using both:

```
LOCAL PROCEDURE FindLastSalesInvoicePrice(ItemNo : Code[20]) : Decimal;
VAR
  ValueEntry : Record 5802;
BEGIN
  ValueEntry.SETCURRENTKEY("Item No.","Posting Date");
  ValueEntry.SETRANGE("Item No.",ItemNo);
  ValueEntry.SETRANGE("Entry Type",ValueEntry."Entry Type"::"Direct
  Cost");
  ValueEntry.SETRANGE("Item Ledger Entry Type",ValueEntry."Item Ledger
  Entry Type"::Sale);
  ValueEntry.SETFILTER("Sales Amount (Actual)",'>0');
  ValueEntry.SETFILTER("Valued Quantity",'<0');
  IF ValueEntry.FINDLAST THEN
    EXIT(ROUND(ValueEntry."Sales Amount (Actual)" / ValueEntry."Valued
    Quantity",GetUnitAmountRoundingPrecision));

  EXIT(0);
END;
```

The ValueEntry table keeps a record of item cost and sales prices; this is the table where we can find all amounts related to an item. To find specific records for the given item in a limited period, we use SETRANGE or SETFILTER to exclude records that we don't need from the scope. As the code sample demonstrates, SETRANGE is employed to apply a precise filter value, while SETFILTER can be used to filter with more flexible conditions, such as less than, greater than, or not equal to.

Even with all filters applied, there can be more than one record satisfying the search criteria. Since we are interested in finding only the last one, we call FINDLAST instead of FINDSET, which we used before. FINDLAST will retrieve only the last record from the filtered set and generally works faster than FINDSET when only a single record is required. Similarly, the first record in the dataset is retrieved with the FINDFIRST function. To specify the order in which the recordset must be sorted prior to finding the first or the last record, the SETCURRENTKEY function is called. The resulting set will be sorted according to the list of fields specified in its parameters:

```
LOCAL PROCEDURE SalesInPastMonthExist(ItemNo : Code[20]) : Boolean;
VAR
  ItemLedgerEntry : Record 32;
```

```
BEGIN
  ItemLedgerEntry.SETRANGE("Item No.",ItemNo);
  ItemLedgerEntry.SETRANGE("Entry Type",ItemLedgerEntry."Entry
  Type"::Sale);
  ItemLedgerEntry.SETFILTER(
    "Document Type",
    '%1|%2',
    ItemLedgerEntry."Document Type"::"Sales Invoice",
    ItemLedgerEntry."Document Type"::"Sales Shipment");
  ItemLedgerEntry.SETRANGE("Posting
  Date",CALCDATE('<-1M>',WORKDATE),WORKDATE);
  EXIT(NOT ItemLedgerEntry.ISEMPTY);
END;
```

The `SalesInPastMonthExist` function shows yet another example of how else `SETFILTER` can be used to vary the set of record filters. Here, we pass a set of placeholders as the second parameter of the function. At runtime, the `'%1|%2'` placeholders will be replaced with the exact values that follow. In this case, these values are `Sales Invoice` and `Sales Shipment`. So, finally, the `SETFILTER` with these parameters is going to be interpreted as `Document Type` either equal to `Sales Invoice` or `Sales Shipment`. The `|` symbol means logical *or* in such filters.

Finally, the function checks whether a value satisfying all conditions exists. In order to do this, we call `ISEMPTY`. Instead of actually retrieving the record, `ISEMPTY` performs an index seek. It works faster than `FINDSET` or `FINDFIRST`, since it does not have to look in the table data providing a suitable index exists in the table:

```
LOCAL PROCEDURE GetUnitAmountRoundingPrecision() : Decimal;
VAR
  GLSetup : Record "General Ledger Setup";
BEGIN
  GLSetup.GET;
  EXIT(GLSetup."Unit-Amount Rounding Precision");
END;
```

And, finally, `GetUnitAmountRoundingPrecision` shows one more way of retrieving a record from a table. When you need to find a record by the primary key, there is no need to apply filters. `GET` accepts a list of primary key fields in parameters and retrieves the record. To read all data related to the LS-S15 item, just use Item.GET('LS-S15'). It's still the same if the table has a compound primary key. The unit of measure for the same item is retrieved with the statement ItemUnitOfMeasure.GET('LS-S15','PCS'), assuming that ItemUnitOfMeasure is a Record variable referring to the Item Unit of Measure table.

In the previous example, GET is called without any parameters though. This is because it is applied to the General Ledger Setup table. This table, as with any other setup table, always contains a single record with an empty string for the primary key. So, calling GET without parameters is equivalent to GET('').

Inserting and modifying records

So far, we have dealt with finding required records from a database table. Now let's implement the last part of the exercise and update the retrieved records:

```
LOCAL PROCEDURE SetSalesLineDiscountForItem(ItemNo : Code[20];UnitPrice :
Decimal;StartingDate : Date;EndingDate : Date);
VAR
  SalesPrice : Record "Sales Price";
  RecordFound : Boolean;
BEGIN
  SalesPrice.VALIDATE("Item No.",ItemNo);
  SalesPrice.VALIDATE("Sales Type",SalesPrice."Sales Type"::"All
Customers");
  SalesPrice.VALIDATE("Starting Date",StartingDate);
  RecordFound := SalesPrice.FIND;

  SalesPrice.VALIDATE("Unit Price",UnitPrice);
  SalesPrice.VALIDATE("Ending Date",EndingDate);
  IF RecordFound THEN
    SalesPrice.MODIFY(TRUE)
  ELSE
    SalesPrice.INSERT(TRUE);
END;
```

Here, we fill in a record in the Sales Price table with new values, setting the item to which the new price applies, a customer category to which it applies, starting and ending dates, and the price amount.

To assign values to table fields, we do not use the customary assignment statement, but call the VALIDATE trigger instead. This trigger is executed before the value is assigned to the field, and usually contains code verifying the correctness of the assignment. We will delve into the details of implementing validations in the next chapter.

The last thing the function does before exiting is the insertion or modification of a record, depending on whether it already exists in the database or not. If the record was found, it will be updated with new values. Otherwise, a new record will be inserted.

Codeunit variables – calling functions from other codeunits

In all code examples in this chapter, we created codeunits that contained functions used locally by codeunits themselves. But a codeunit is a code library that could contain common functionality available to other objects. The following section will show how to invoke functions from code libraries in C/AL:

```
LOCAL ExportPriceList(FileName : Text)
    XMLDoc := XMLDoc.XmlDocument;
    XMLDOMManagement.AddRootElement(XMLDoc,'PriceList',RootNode);
    IF Item.FINDSET THEN
        REPEAT
XMLDOMManagement.AddElement(RootNode,'Item',Item."No.",'',ItemNode);
XMLDOMManagement.AddAttribute(ItemNode,'Description',Item.Description);
XMLDOMManagement.AddAttribute(ItemNode,'Price',FORMAT(Item."Unit Price"));
        UNTIL Item.NEXT = 0;

    F.CREATE(FileName);
    F.CREATEOUTSTREAM(XmlOutStream);
    XMLDoc.Save(XmlOutStream);
    F.CLOSE;
```

This code snippet introduces a new variable type never used in previous examples, `DotNet`. Here, we create an XML document as an instance of a .NET class, `XmlDocument`, and two instances of the `XmlNode` class for XML nodes. In NAV, variables of type `DotNet` refer to .NET classes and give access to their functions the same way any other .NET language would do.

To declare a `DotNet` variable, you need to select the `DotNet` type name from the **DataType** drop-down list, then choose an assembly and a class or an interface name.

Here is how we declare an `XmlDocument` variable:

1. In the `ExportPriceList` function, open the Locals window and switch to the **Variables** tab.
2. In the **Name** field, enter the name of the variable, `XmlDoc`, then choose **DotNet** in the **DataType**.

3. Click on the assist button in **Subtype** field; this will open a new window, .NET Type List. But so far, you don't see any .NET types in the list—it is empty. Click the lookup button in the **Assembly** field to select a .NET assembly first. This action will show the list of all available .NET assemblies. Switch to the tab titled .NET and select System.Xml from the list of assemblies:

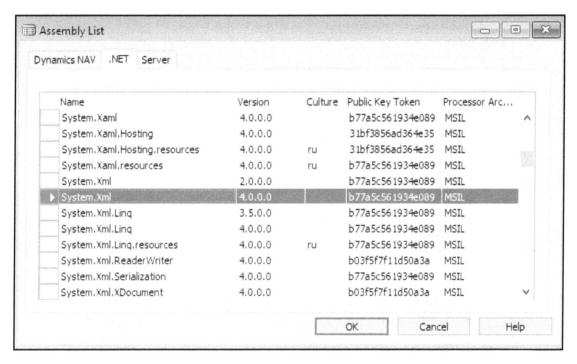

List of .NET assemblies

4. Click **OK**; you will return to the **.NET** type list window, but this will show all .NET types available in the System.Xml assembly.

5. Choose **System.Xml.XmlDocument**, then click **OK**:

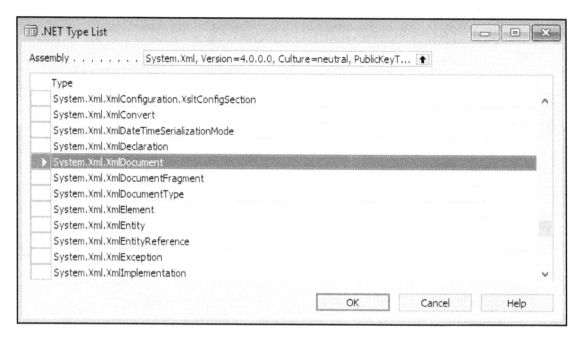

.NET types exported from the selected assembly

This completes the variable declaration. Now declare two other local `DotNet` variables: `RootNode` and `ItemNode`, both with `System.Xml.XmlNode` for the subtype.

So, finally, the list of local variables for `ExportPriceList` should look like this:

```
Item : Record 27;
XMLDOMManagement : Codeunit 6224;
XMLDoc : DotNet "System.Xml.XmlDocument";
RootNode : DotNet "System.Xml.XmlNode";
ItemNode : DotNet "System.Xml.XmlNode";
XmlOutStream : OutStream;
F : File;
```

`DotNet` variables are different from other NAV data types in the way that they are not immediately instantiated after declaration. An instance of a .NET class must be created explicitly by calling its constructor, and this is the first thing we do in the `ExportPriceList` function:

```
XMLDoc := XMLDoc.XmlDocument;
```

After this line, the `XMLDoc` variable is accessible in the code.

We do not explicitly invoke constructors on `RootNode` and `ItemNode`, because this is done inside the `XMLDOMManagement.AddElement` function.

The `ExportPriceList` function exports table data into an XML file on the server. Users need this file on the client side to be able to work with it, so in the next step, this file must be downloaded to the client. Before copying the file, we will also pack it into a zip archive. All these actions are performed using functions from the `FileManagement` library. Function archiving and downloading the file are in the following code block:

```
LOCAL PROCEDURE ZipAndDownloadFile@7(ServerFileName : Text);
VAR
  ZipFileName : Text;
  ClientFileName : Text;
BEGIN
  ZipFileName:= FileManagement.CreateZipArchiveObject;
  FileManagement.AddFileToZipArchive(ServerFileName,STRSUBSTNO('PriceList -
%1.txt',WORKDATE));
  FileManagement.CloseZipArchive;
  ClientFileName := FileManagement.SaveFileDialog('Save File','','ZIP
archive|*.zip');
  FileManagement.DownloadToFile(ZipFileName,ClientFileName);

  FileManagement.DeleteServerFile(ServerFileName);
  FileManagement.DeleteServerFile(ZipFileName);
END;
```

To run all the code, invoke both functions from the `OnRun` trigger, as shown in the next code block:

```
OnRun()
    ServerFileName := FileManagement.ServerTempFileName('xml');
    ExportPriceList(ServerFileName);
    ZipAndDownloadFile(ServerFileName);
```

Text constants

Text constants in C/AL are declared the same way as variables: through the C/AL Locals or C/AL Globals editors. In most cases, constants are declared as globals. It is good practice to avoid global variables when a local one is sufficient, but this is not the case with constants. A global variable often causes specific bugs; since it is available in any part of the code, and any function can change its value, it becomes very difficult to track the value of the variable while the volume of the code grows. This is not a problem with constants, because once assigned, the value of a constant cannot be changed.

With this in mind, in all code samples where text constants are involved, we will declare them as globals. A typical application of text constants is UI messages: process information or error notifications. And having a constant in the global scope is handy when you need to show the same message in different parts of the application.

To demonstrate the application of text constants, we will write a function that checks for overdue sales invoices and shows an appropriate message, depending on the result. This function is going to be placed in a new codeunit, so first of all, create one.

Declaring text constants is very similar to declaring functions or variables. To declare a global text constant, follow these steps:

1. In the C/SIDE code editor, select the **View | Globals** menu action.
2. Select the **Text Constants** tab in the C/AL Globals form.
3. Enter the name of the constant in the **Name** field, and its value in the **ConstValue** field.

For this example, declare two constants in the codeunit you just created:

```
OverdueCountMsg : TextConst 'ENU=There are %1 overdue invoices on %2';
NoOverdueInvoicesMsg : TextConst 'ENU=All customer invoices are paid';
```

Besides two text constants, the following local variables should be declared in the function:

```
CustLedgerEntry : Record 21;
OverdueInvoicesCount : Integer;
```

Here is how we use the constants:

```
OnRun()
    CustLedgerEntry.SETRANGE("Document Type",CustLedgerEntry."Document
Type"::Invoice);
    CustLedgerEntry.SETFILTER("Due Date",'<%1',WORKDATE);
    CustLedgerEntry.SETRANGE(Open,TRUE);
    OverdueInvoicesCount := CustLedgerEntry.COUNT;
    IF OverdueInvoicesCount > 0 THEN
        MESSAGE(OverdueCountMsg,OverdueInvoicesCount,WORKDATE)
    ELSE
        MESSAGE(NoOverdueInvoicesMsg);
```

If there are no unpaid overdue invoices on the WORKDATE, this function displays a message box with text from the NoOverdueInvoicesMsg text constant. Otherwise, the other constant, OverdueCountMsg, will be used.

Typically, the text constant is a part of a dialog text displayed to the user with one of the functions MESSAGE, ERROR, CONFIRM, or STRMENU. Note that the OverdueCountMsg text constant contains placeholders that should be replaced with actual values at runtime. The MESSAGE function, as well as ERROR and CONFIRM, do this substitution and do not require the string parameter to be formatted with STRSUBSTNO.

Summary

The second chapter gave a more detailed overview of a topic started in Chapter 1, *Getting Started with the NAV Development Environment*. We learned to create codeunits, structure C/AL code into functions, pass parameters to functions, and use return values. The first examples illustrating C/SIDE capabilities were of a somewhat abstract nature, but closer to the end of the chapter, we learned how to use the database and discussed a more business-related scenario.

In the following chapter, readers will not only learn to use Record variables, but will complete a walk-through example of creating a custom table and writing table triggers.

3
Tables - Creating Data Structure

ERP is all about data. Any document created in the system, any activity recorded, financial entries, and today's currency exchange rates—are all records in the database. When it comes to rendering a VAT statement report or building a sales forecast for the next quarter, the quality, precision, and performance of these reports depend on the underlying data.

In this and the following chapters, we will develop a simple but fully functional solution in C/AL, integrated with the base NAV application. And now, we are going to begin with the most important part of the application, the data structure.

In this chapter, you will learn how to create tables in Dynamics NAV, from defining fields to writing triggers in C/AL. This chapter covers the following topics:

- Designing the table structure
- Synchronizing the table metadata with SQL Server
- Defining the primary key and secondary indexes
- Configuring the default pages for tables
- Table relations
- Field class: Flowfields and Flowfilters
- Table triggers
- `Rec` and `xRec` global variables

Designing the table structure

NAV table objects are mapped to actual database tables; for each table in NAV, there is a corresponding table in the SQL Server database, and the NAV table designer is an interface for constructing table metadata that will be represented in database table fields.

The first table we will create is the contract header containing general information related to the contract: contract number, customer, and starting and ending dates.

Creating tables

To create a table, open the Object Designer and switch to the **Table** view; press the **Table** button in the left pane of the designer window. In the **Table Designer**, we create the new table by describing its fields line by line with the following metadata values:

- **Enabled**: Indicates whether this field is created in the corresponding SQL database table. If the field is disabled, it is not mapped to the database. The default value of this option is **true**, and we are not going to change this.
- **Field No**: As with any other object in NAV, fields are identified by their numbers, along with names. This is an internal identifier that does not affect data storage. The only requirement is that this ID must be unique within the table.
- **Field Name**: Human-readable field name that clearly reflects its purpose and is used in C/AL code as the field identifier.
- **Data Type**: Type of data that will be stored in this field. We will familiarize ourselves with the most essential data types in this chapter.
- **Length**: Applicable for text data types (text and code) and binary data. The maximum length of the string that can be stored in this field. Maximum possible length is 250.
- **Description**: A text comment describing the field.
- **Field Class:** This is an option that can take one of three values: **Normal**, **FlowField**, or **FlowFilter**. Only **Normal** fields are stored in the database, and these are mapped to table fields in SQL. The two other classes are special types of fields supporting dynamic data aggregation. We will learn how to use these fields later in this chapter.

This is not a complete list of field properties, but only the values shown in the table designer interface with default settings. To access other properties, select the field and choose the **View** | **Properties** menu action, or press *Shift + F4*.

Let's create the first of the tables required for the leasing payments solution. **Propertied Enabled** and **Field Class** always receive default values, and other properties should be filled in as shown in the table:

Table **50500 Lease Contract Header**:

Field no.	Field name	Data type	Length
1	No.	Code	20
2	Customer No.	Code	20
3	Starting Date	Date	
4	Ending Date	Date	

When you are done defining the table structure, save the table.

A table must contain at least one field. Tables without any fields defined in their design cannot be saved.

The second table, **Lease Contract Line**, will store document lines. It is defined the same way as the header table: create a new table and the following fields to the table design:

Field no.	Field name	Data type	Length
1	Contract No.	Code	20
2	Line No.	Integer	
3	Item No.	Code	20
4	Description	Text	50
5	Amount	Decimal	

The first field of the **Contract No.** table will refer to the contract header. Further on in this chapter, we will see how to set up this relation. **Line No.** identifies the particular line of the contract, and **Item No.** is the item in the lease.

Besides the contract header and its lines, we will store the log of customer payments associated with contracts. For this purpose, we are going to create one more table, **Customer Payment**. In the table designer, create a table object with fields listed as follows:

Field no.	Field name	Data type	Length
1	Entry No.	Integer	
2	Contract No.	Code	20
3	Contract Line No.	Integer	
4	Payment Date	Date	

5	Amount	Decimal	
6	Invoice Created	Boolean	
7	Global Dimension 1 Code	Code	20
8	Global Dimension 2 Code	Code	20
9	Customer Group Code	Code	20
10	Salesperson Code	Code	20

Synchronizing table metadata with SQL Server

As mentioned earlier, every table object in Dynamics NAV has its counterpart in SQL Server: a physical database table that stores the data. There are exceptions to this rule, called virtual tables, which will be explained later in this book. But every table created by C/AL developers inevitably triggers synchronization of its metadata with SQL Server. This means that the NAV server, as well as C/SIDE, operates an internal snapshot of table metadata, which is stored separately from SQL Server metadata and must be synchronized when changes occur.

When you saved the tables created in the previous section of this chapter, you may have noticed that the **Save As** dialog looks different than the same dialog for Codeunits. When a table is saved, it has one addition parameter, **Synchronize Schema**. The next screenshot shows the **Save as** dialog for a table:

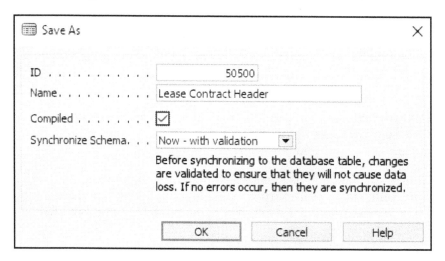

Save As dialog

Saving a table triggers the synchronization of metadata between Dynamics NAV and SQL Server, and the **Synchronize Schema** parameter defines the synchronization method. So far, we have not paid any attention to this field, because its default value works perfectly well for new tables. It will not affect your development experience if you decide to extend a table by adding new fields. This option comes into play when an existing table field is changed or deleted.

When implementing schema synchronization, the NAV server verifies field modification to identify potential destructive changes. A change is considered destructive if it can potentially damage table data when carried out.

Examples of destructive changes are as follows:

- Table is deleted
- Table field is deleted
- Length of a text field is reduced
- Data type of a field is changed, and implicit conversion is impossible (for example, data type changed from **Text** to **Integer** or vice versa)
- Field is removed from a compound primary key

If the server detects a destructive change, it looks for upgrade triggers defining data conversion procedures. If no such triggers are found, the table is not saved, and the action fails with an error message: **The schema synchronization may result in deleted data**. So, if you see this error message when you save your table, most likely one of the preceding changes took place.

C/SIDE gives us three options for schema synchronization:

- **Now-with validation**: All modifications in the table design are reflected in SQL tables immediately.
- **Later**: Synchronization of metadata is postponed. Changes are saved in the NAV data, but the server runs on the old version of the table. Synchronization must be done manually.
- **Force**: Metadata is synchronized immediately, but the validation of changes is skipped. Any destructive changes are applied without running upgrade procedures.

The force option is intended for development and test environments, and should not be used in a production database, as this may result in data corruption.

Defining the primary key and secondary indexes

We created several tables in previous sections, but never defined primary keys. This means that the development environment decided which fields to use for primary keys for us. In C/SIDE, the first field in the table automatically becomes its primary key and the clustered index. Now we will review and adjust primary keys and define indexes that will help us improve application performance.

Defining primary keys

When a new table is created, the primary key is created automatically by the Object Designer. The first field defined in the table is assigned as the single primary key field. This is not always the primary key the developer means for the table. Let's see how to change the primary key manually.

Review the **Lease Contract Header** table and look at the primary key suggested by the Object Designer. To access the table keys, open the table in the Object Designer and choose the **View | Keys** menu action.

This action will show the list of table keys. There is only one key with a single field number in it. This is what we want for the **Lease Contract Header**, so now close the keys list and the table designer to return to the **Object Designer** interface.

The field **Contract No.** is also automatically set as the primary key for the **Lease Contract Line** table. In this case, though, a single field is insufficient to identify records. The **Line No.** field must be included in the primary key as well, so now we need to change the primary key structure. To modify a table key, follow these steps:

1. Open the list of table keys, as described previously.
2. Select the **Key** field in the **Keys** table.
3. Press the assist button. This action opens the list of fields included in the selected key.
4. Using the lookup button, select all fields that need to be in the key.

Following this action list, extend the primary key of the **Lease Contract Line** table, so that it includes two fields: **Contract No.** and **Line No.**. The following screenshot illustrates the **Keys** window and the key setup:

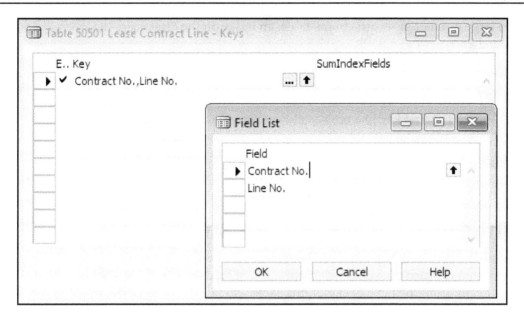

Compound primary key

Finally, the **Customer Payment** table has a primary key consisting of one field, **Entry No.**, automatically assigned to it. This is exactly what we need; there is no need to change the key of this table.

Table indexes

All table keys except the primary key are mapped to indexes in the corresponding SQL Server table. While not mandatory, indexes help improve the performance of queries against the table. It is a good idea to declare an index on fields that are often used in search criteria on the table. For example, the **Lease Contract Header** table has a field, **Customer No.**. It is likely that we will use this field for filtering to find all contracts for a certain customer. Probably,we don't even want to select all contracts belonging to a customer, but only active ones. In this case, we will run code similar to this:

```
LeaseContractHeader.SETRANGE("Customer No.",'10000');
LeaseContractHeader.SETFILTER("Starting Date",'<=',WORKDATE);
LeaseContractHeader.SETFILTER("Ending Date",'>=',WORKDATE);
LeaseContractHeader.FINDSET;
```

With a large number of records in the table, an index on the `Customer No.`, `Starting Date`, and `Ending Date` fields will boost the query.

To create a secondary index on a table, follow the same steps as for declaring the primary key.

 The first key in a table is always the primary key; all the other keys are created in the corresponding SQL table as indexes.

Configuring default pages for tables

Although the user interface is a topic for the next chapter, where it will be covered in detail, now we need to touch on some basic techniques of UI design. C/SIDE allows us to run tables directly from the table designer, the same way we did with Codeunits. But it's always a good practice to create at least one page for any new table that is supposed to present data to the user. Some types of tables may have more than one page associated with them, but right now, we will create one list page to represent contracts.

Creating a list page using a page wizard

Now we will complete a simple walk-through to create a list page for the table. The following steps provide the details of creating a list page using the page wizard:

1. In the C/SIDE Object Designer, select the **Page** icon.
2. Press the **New** button to open the **New Page** dialog window.
3. In the **New Page** dialog, enter the ID or name of the table in the **Table** field.
4. Select the **Create a page using a wizard** option and choose **List** from the list of templates:

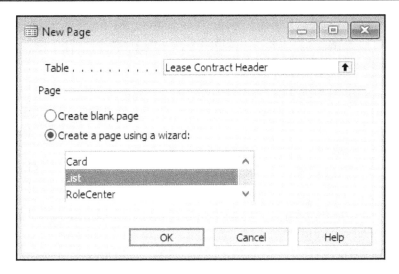

New page setup

5. Click **OK** and you will be redirected to the **List page** creation wizard, where you can choose which fields should appear on the page.
6. Select all suggested fields and press **Finish**.
7. Save the new page as 50500 Lease Contracts Header.

Now, you can run the new page from the Object Designer and review the layout, although the underlying table still has no data to display.

Configuring default lookup and drilldown pages

In the following sections of this chapter, we will learn how to look up records in related tables and drill down from calculated fields into underlying data. For these functions to work, default lookup and drilldown pages must be set up for the table. To configure default pages, follow these steps:

1. Open the **50500 Lease Contract Header** table, in the table designer.
2. Select a blank line under the last field.
3. Select the **View | Properties** action. Make sure that the cursor is positioned below all table fields, otherwise field properties will be displayed instead of table properties.

4. Choose the **LookupPageID** property and enter the ID of list page 50500.
5. Enter the same page **ID** for the **DrillDownPageID** property.
6. Close the table properties and save changes.

Now you have completed a preparation step to incorporate lookup functionality into your application. The next section will guide you through the development of this function.

Table relations

Table lookups are everywhere in NAV. You create a sales order and select a customer from a list of all customers in the system. When you add a line to the order, you use lookups to choose an item, location, and item unit of measure. Any time you select a value from a lookup list, most likely there is a table relation behind this selection.

The following example shows how to set up a table relation for the **Customer No.** field in the **Lease Contract Header** table. This configuration will enable page lookup functionality and help the user easily select a customer from a contract:

1. Open the **50500 Lease Contract Header** table, in the table designer.
2. Select the **Customer No.** field and navigate to its properties (**View | Properties**).
3. Enter the table name, Customer, in the **TableRelation** property. The table ID can be used instead of the name; it does not matter whether you enter 18 or Customer.

To see how it works, run the **Lease Contracts** page and create a new contract record. Enter the contract number in the **No.** field, then move to the **Customer No.** field. This field now has a lookup button. When pressed, this button opens a list of customers, where you can select one or create a new record and assign it to the contract. In the following screenshot, you can see an example of the table lookup:

Field lookup

Table relations configured this way enable the user to see all records in the related table and select a value from the list. But often the list of acceptable values should be limited based on some filtering criteria. For example, the **Customer Payment** table, which we created earlier in this chapter, has two fields referring to dimension values. These are Global Dimension 1 code and Global Dimension 2 code. When opening a lookup list from these two fields, we don't want to see all dimension values, but expect the list to be limited to respective dimension code, **Global Dimension 1 Code** or **Global Dimension 2 Code**. The following walk-through demonstrates how to set up a filtered table relationship:

1. Open **50502 Customer Payment** table, in the table designer.
2. Select the **Global Dimension 1 Code** field.
3. Open the field's properties and navigate to the **TableRelation** property. Do not enter the table name or ID here, but click the assist button in the property value instead.

The **Table Relation** editor window that opens now has four columns, of which only **Table** is required to set up a relation; the other parameters are optional. For our configuration, we will need three parameters: **Table**, **Field**, and **Table Filter**. Follow these steps to set up the table relation:

1. Enter the table name, **Dimension Value,** in the **Table** field. It can be table ID 349, the same as in the previous example.
2. For the **Field** property, enter the field name **Code**, or press the lookup button and choose the field from the list.
3. In the **Table Filter** field, press the assist button, which will open yet another editor window, dedicated to configuring the filter for the lookup list.
4. Fill the table filter fields as follows: **Field = Global Dimension No.**, **Type = CONST**, and **Value = 1**, as shown in the following screenshot:

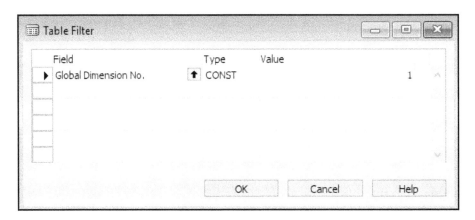

Configuring a filter for table relations

After completing the filter setup, click **OK** in the open windows, **Table Filter** then **Table Relation**, close the field properties, and save the table.

 Be sure to confirm your changes with the **OK** button. If you simply close the page, all changes will be lost.

This scenario introduces two differences compared to the first example in this section. First, we explicitly specify the field in the **Dimension Value** table that is used in the relationship. This is required, because **Dimension Value** has a compound primary key consisting of two fields: **Dimension Code** and **Code**. In this case, we must be specific about the field we want to refer to.

The second difference is the filter applied on the **Dimension Value** table when the lookup is activated.

Field class – Flowfields and Flowfilters

In previous sections of this chapter, we created several tables, all of them containing fields that stored some data and were mapped to fields in corresponding tables in SQL Server. Besides these data fields, C/SIDE has two field types that are not stored in the SQL database, but help in calculating aggregated values from other tables. Now we will see how to create and configure fields called FlowFields and FlowFilters.

Modifying FieldClass

The property **FieldClass** defines how the table field can be used by the client application. Possible values of the property are explained as follows:

- **Normal**: This is the usual field that contains table data. So far, we have worked only with normal fields.
- **FlowField**: Aggregated field, which is calculated from other fields. The value of the FlowField is not stored in the database, but calculated by the NAV server at runtime.
- **FlowFilter**: Similar to FlowField, the FlowFilter field does not exist in the SQL database. These fields are used as a part of the calculation formula for FlowFields to filter the records included in the calculation. In RTC, when you open the **Limit totals to** section on any page, you see the list of FlowFilters.

Now we will create a calculated field in the **Lease Contract Header** table to sum up the total amount in contract lines, and include a FlowFilter to enable filtering on the specific item in the contract.

Add another field to the **50500 Lease Contract Header** table. Properties that should be assigned to the new field are in the next table:

Field no.	Field name	Data type
5	Total Amount	Decimal

In the **FieldClass** field, which we have not changed so far, select the **FlowField** field class from the drop-down list. Since FlowFields only display the calculation result and do not store the data, they should not accept user input. To make the field not editable, change the value of the field's **Editable** property to **No**.

Add one more field to the same table, **50500 Lease Contract Header,** with parameters as in the following table:

Field no.	Field name	Data type	Length
6	Item No. Filter	Code	20

For this field, change the **FieldClass** from the default **Normal** to **FlowFilter**.

Also, the field **Item No. Filter** must allow a lookup to the Item table, so open the field properties and set the value of the **TableRelation** property to **Item**. Configured this way, the **Item No. Filter** field will reference the primary key of the Item table, allowing lookups on the referenced table.

In the next step, we will configure the calculation formula for the new FlowField. This formula is going to rely on the FlowFilter Item No. Filter to specify which items should be included in the calculation. In order to set up the formula, we need to save the table design, close the designer, and reopen it again. If you attempt to set up the calculation rules right away, new fields will not be available in the formula configuration designer.

Configuring the field calculation formula

After you have saved and reopened the table design, you can make the next step and set up the FlowField's calculation formula. To access the formula designer, follow these steps:

1. Open the **50500 Lease Contract Header** table, in the table designer.
2. Select the **Total Amount** field and navigate to its properties (**View** | **Properties**).
3. Press the assist button next to the **CalcFormula** property.

This action button opens a window where you can configure a formula to calculate the value of the **Total Amount** field. Here, you specify the aggregation function that is used to calculate the amount, the related table, and a field in it from which the value is computed.

Set the following values for these fields:

- **Method**: Sum
- **Table**: Lease Contract Line
- **Field**: Amount

This setup means that the calculation algorithm will summarize the field amount in all records in the **Lease Contract Line** table. But we don't want to sum all records; we need to limit the amount to a specific contract and item. To exclude records that we don't want in the result, a table filter must be configured. Press the assist button in the **Table Filter** field and set up the filter as shown in the following screenshot:

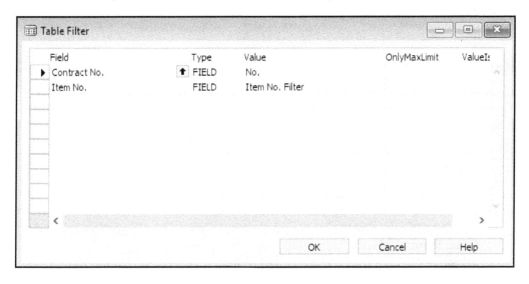

Configuring table filters for a FlowField calculation formula

When the filter setup is done, press **OK** in the **Table Filter** window to save the filter and return to the calculation formula configuration. The formula setup window should now look as in the following screenshot:

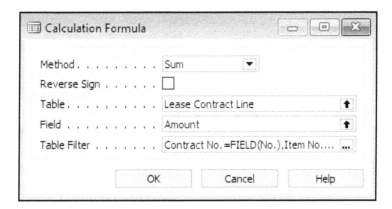

FlowField calculation formula

And here is the complete **Table Filter** line:

```
Sum("Lease Contract Line".Amount WHERE (Contract No.=FIELD(No.),Item
No.=FIELD(Item No. Filter)))
```

This completes the setup of the FlowField **Total Amount**. To see how it works, we need one more step: display the field on the page.

Adding a field to a page

We already created a list page to display all contracts, which we can extend with the additional field, **Total Amount**. The following short walk-through illustrates the steps to add a new field to a page:

1. Select the **50500 Lease Contracts** page, in the page designer and press **Design**; the list of page fields will be displayed.
2. Navigate to a blank line, below the last line of the page designer.
3. Position the cursor in the field **SourceExpr** and press the assist button if this field (or alternatively, use the keyboard shortcut *Shift + F2*). This action opens the **C/AL Symbol Menu**.
4. To select the field that is to be added to the page, first choose the **Rec** variable, **FieldName**, and the **Total Amount** field in three panes of the C/AL Symbol Menu. The following screenshot shows the **C/AL Symbol Menu**, where you can select a field that should be added to the page:

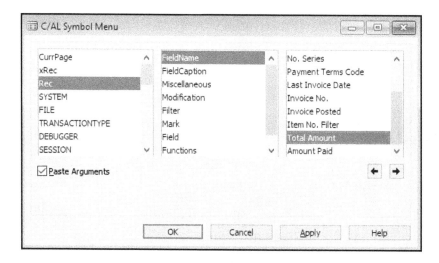

Selecting data source for a page field

After configuring the data source, press **OK** and save the changes in the page design.

Further into the book, we will need one more FlowField in **50500 Lease Contract Header** table. This field will be used to calculate the amount paid by the customer per contract. Data for the calculation is stored in the **Customer Payment** table. Add the field to the table as shown:

Field no.	Field name	Data type	Field Class
7	Amount Paid	Decimal	FlowField

Following the steps in this section, set up the calculation formula to match the following code:

```
Sum("Customer Payment".Amount WHERE (Contract No.=FIELD(No.)))
```

Or else, just copy the formula to the field's `CalcFormula` property.

Table triggers

A table trigger is a C/AL function that is called by the NAV platform in response to certain events in the table, such as inserting or modifying a record, or entering a value in a table field. The key difference between a common C/AL function and a table trigger is that the latter cannot be called explicitly in application code; it is either initiated by user actions or called implicitly when other C/AL functions perform data manipulations on the table.

Then, we will implement several examples of table triggers bound to different actions on a table. The first example is the `OnDelete` trigger, invoked when a table record is being deleted. This trigger will delete all contract lines when the contract is deleted.

Open the **50500 Lease Contract Header** table, in table designer and find the `OnDelete` trigger declaration. It has already been generated by the designer, so developers don't have to declare the triggers they intend to use.

In the `OnDelete` trigger, declare a local variable, `LeaseContractLine : Record "Lease Contract Line"`.

Write the code shown here, which will delete linked lines on deleting a contract header:

```
LeaseContractLine.SETRANGE("Contract No.","No.");
LeaseContractLine.DELETEALL(TRUE);
```

The `OnDelete` trigger is called by the NAV platform when a user deletes a table record, or the `DELETE` function is called from the application code. But note that the C/AL functions `DELETE`, `INSERT`, and `MODIFY` invoke the corresponding triggers `OnDelete`, `OnInsert`, and `OnModify` only if called with the optional parameter `RunTrigger = TRUE`. To run the previous trigger , we need to call a line, `LeaseContractHeader.DELETE(TRUE)`. `LeaseContractHeader.DELETE` will delete the contract header, but will not run the trigger and the contract lines will not be deleted.

Another example of a commonly used table trigger is the `OnLookup` trigger. Unlike the previously discussed `OnInsert`, `OnDelete`, and `OnModify` triggers, which are not bound to any field in particular, `OnLookup` is associated with a field rather than the whole record. It is typically used to run a lookup action more complex than the simple **TableRelation** property allows. The `OnLookup` trigger enables developers to achieve more flexible behavior for lookups controlled through C/AL code. To run a lookup from the trigger, let's first write a function that will be called from the trigger and open the lookup page. We will look up dimension values in table **50501 Customer Payment**. The following code block presents a function, `LookupDimensionValue`, that should be created in table **50502 Customer Payment**:

```
LOCAL PROCEDURE LookupDimensionValue(VAR SelectedValue : Code[20];LookupDim
: Option) : Boolean;
VAR
    DimensionValue : Record 349;
    UserAction : Action;
BEGIN
    SetDimensionCodeFilter(DimensionValue,LookupDim);
    UserAction := PAGE.RUNMODAL(0,DimensionValue);
    SelectedValue := DimensionValue.Code;
    EXIT(UserAction = ACTION::LookupOK);
END;
```

After applying filters on the **Dimension Value** table, we pass it to `PAGE.RUNMODAL` to show the table in a modal page. The value returned from the function is the action that the user selects on the page (push the **OK** or **Cancel** button).

 Application code in the `OnLookup` trigger overrides the lookup rules configured in the `TableRelation` property for the same field. If the trigger contains any code, the property value is ignored.

For the following function, we will need two global variables to be declared in the **Customer Payment** table. Create the variables as per this table:

Name	Data type	Subtype
SalesSetup	Record	Sales and Receivables Setup
LookupOption	Option	

`LookupOption` is the option type variable and requires the option string to be defined. Open the variable properties and add the value for the `OptionString` property: `CustomerGroup,Salesperson`.

The next code block presents the `SetDimensionCodeFilter` function, which sets filters on the lookup table. The new thing here is the use of filter groups. The `FILTERGROUP` function sets the active group in which subsequent filters will be applied. Normally, filters available to be used in the UI are applied in filter group 0. Groups with higher numbers are reserved for system use, but they are available to developers as well to set filters hidden from the UI, and which the user cannot edit:

```
LOCAL PROCEDURE SetDimensionCodeFilter(
  VAR DimensionValue : Record 349;DimensionOption : Option);
BEGIN
  SalesSetup.GET;

  DimensionValue.FILTERGROUP(2);
  CASE DimensionOption OF
    LookupOption::CustomerGroup:
      DimensionValue.SETRANGE("Dimension Code",SalesSetup."Customer Group
Dimension Code");
    LookupOption::Salesperson:
      DimensionValue.SETRANGE("Dimension Code",SalesSetup."Salesperson
Dimension Code");
  END;
  DimensionValue.FILTERGROUP(0);
END;
```

 The last filter group selected for the table before showing it in the UI remains active in the page. Don't forget to switch the filter group back to 0 before calling `PAGE.RUN` or `PAGE.RUNMODAL`. Otherwise, users will be able to see and edit filters in the last selected group.

To complete the example, call the `LookupDimensionValue` function from the `OnLookup` trigger of the `Customer Group Code` field, as shown in this code block:

```
OnLookup
VAR
  NewValue : Code[20];
BEGIN
  IF LookupDimensionValue(NewValue,LookupOption::CustomerGroup) THEN
    "Customer Group Code" := NewValue;
END;
```

The same should be done for the `Salesperson Code` field. See the following code block for an example:

```
OnLookup=VAR
  NewValue : Code[20];
BEGIN
  IF LookupDimensionValue(NewValue,LookupOption::CustomerGroup) THEN
    "Salesperson Code" := NewValue;
END;
```

Similar to the `OnLookup` trigger, `OnValidate` is fired in response to user actions in a specific record field. `OnValidate` reacts to the user input in the table and is called after the value is entered, but before it is saved to the database. This trigger is the usual container for code performing input verification. In the same table, **50502 Customer Payment**, create a function, `ValidateDimensionValue`. This will verify the correctness of the manually entered dimension value code. The following is the code of the function:

```
LOCAL PROCEDURE ValidateDimensionValue(EnteredDimValue : Code[20];DimOption
: Option) : Code[20];
VAR
   DimensionValue : Record 349;
BEGIN
   SetDimensionCodeFilter(DimensionValue,DimOption);
   DimensionValue.FINDFIRST;
   DimensionValue.Code := EnteredDimValue;
   DimensionValue.FIND('=>');
   EXIT(DimensionValue.Code);
END;
```

The `ValidateDimensionValue` function catches user input and finds the closest dimension value to the entered one. This action imitates the system behavior when the user inputs a partial value for the dimension code with `TableRelation` enabled, and the NAV platform autocompletes the input. For the customer group dimension, this can be a value, `MED`, that should be resolved to `MEDIUM`.

The function is called from the `Customer Group Code` trigger: `OnValidate` in table **50502 Customer Payment**:

```
"Customer Group Code" := ValidateDimensionValue("Customer Group
Code",LookupOption::CustomerGroup);
```

The same function is called for the dimension `Salesperson Code` in the trigger `Salesperson Code—OnValidate`:

```
"Salesperson Code" := ValidateDimensionValue("Salesperson
Code",LookupOption::Salesperson);
```

In the contract header, we use the same approach to validate the correctness of the starting and ending dates. Create the following function in the **50500 Lease Contract Header** table:

```
LOCAL PROCEDURE ValidateDates();
BEGIN
  IF ("Starting Date" = 0D) OR ("Ending Date" = 0D) THEN
    EXIT;

  IF "Ending Date" < "Starting Date" THEN
    ERROR(WrongStartEndDateErr);
END;
```

This function should be called from the `Starting Date—OnValidate` and `Ending Date—OnValidate` triggers of the **50500 Lease Contract Header** table.

Rec and xRec global variables

In the previous section dedicated to table triggers, we referred to the fields of the current table by simply naming these fields, such as **Starting Date**, **Ending Date**, or **Customer Group Code**. In fact, these fields belong to a global variable, `Rec`, that always exists within the context of a table and refers to the table instance itself. References to table fields are implicitly resolved to `Rec` if the record context is not specified explicitly.

Any data manipulation functions are also applied to the context of the current record instance when called without a variable reference. If, for example, we want to make sure that the user fills the item code in the contract line before specifying the amount, we could do it by calling `TESTFIELD` on the `Item No.` in the context of the current record. Here is the code to do the validation in the the `OnValidate` trigger in table 50501, **Lease Contract Line,** as shown here:

```
Amount - OnValidate()
  TESTFIELD("Item No.");
```

This test will throw an error if the item code in the record being edited is blank.

Another global variable that always exists in the context of the current table is xRec. This variable keeps the state of the record as it appeared before modification occurred.

There may be various situations where the developer wants to know the state of the record before the modification. An example of how this variable can be used is the change in the job status. Base NAV code has many examples illustrating the application of xRec. For instance, of the code samples can be found in the table **Job**, trigger Status—OnValidate:

```
IF xRec.Status = xRec.Status::Completed THEN
   IF DIALOG.CONFIRM(StatusChangeQst) THEN
      VALIDATE(Complete,FALSE)
```

Here, the status of the job is checked before committing the new value selected by the user in the **Status** field. If the job was already completed, confirmation is requested before reopening the closed job. There are numerous examples of the use of this variable, and they will all refer to a record in its previous state.

In our leasing solution, we will employ another pattern involving the use of the xRec variable. When a new contract header is created, by default the number for the new contract is assigned from the same number series that was used for the previous document. xRec."No. Series" is the previously used number series. Code implementing this pattern is shown in the following block. It should be placed in the OnInsert trigger of table **50500 Lease Contract Header**:

```
OnInsert=BEGIN
  SalesSetup.GET;
  IF "No." = '' THEN BEGIN
    SalesSetup.TESTFIELD("Lease Contract Nos.");
    NoSeriesMgt.InitSeries(
      SalesSetup."Lease Contract Nos.",xRec."No. Series","Starting
Date","No.","No. Series");
  END;
END;
```

The current instance of the table can be referred to in C/AL code as Rec. In the preceding line, Starting Date is equivalent to Rec."Starting Date", No. is the same as Rec."No.", and so on.

Summary

This chapter, dedicated to NAV tables, covered the most essential topics related to data structures. It explained how to define table fields, keys, and indexes, and configure virtual fields calculated based on other tables' data. We concluded the chapter with an introduction to C/AL table triggers.

In the next chapter, we will discuss elements of the user interface, such as cards pages, lists pages, subpages, and factboxes. Also, we will introduce the reader to menu suites, objects that structure the user menu.

Designing User Interface

This chapter gives a more in-depth look at the topic briefly started in `Chapter 3`, *Tables - Creating Data Structure*. Here, we will delve deeper into the design of the user interface. The central element of the Dynamics NAV UI is a page, so the chapter is mostly dedicated to different types of pages and their applications. We will see how to create a simple page with several mouse clicks with a page wizard, and learn to build more complex pages with embedded subpages.

Another topic covered in this chapter is C/AL development applied to the UI: how we can enrich pages with C/AL code.

Finally, we will create navigation elements that assist users in finding the required application components: a role center page and a menu suite.

The following topics will be covered in this chapter:

- Page creation wizard
- Card and list pages
- Writing C/AL code in pages
- ListPart and CardPart pages
- Lookups and DrillDowns
- Page action designer
- Role center pages
- Menu suite

Page creation wizard

We will begin our journey to the NAV user interface from the page creation wizard, a tool that allows us to solve most common interface tasks with several mouse clicks. With the page creation wizard, you can create different types of pages based on a table: display table fields on a page, organize them into groups, and categorize them in separate tabs. As we will also see later in this chapter, with the page creation wizard, it is also possible to create more complex UI elements, such as lists, subpages, and FactBoxes, and embed these into the main page.

Card pages

In Chapter 3, *Tables - Creating Data Structure*, we already ran the page creation wizard to create a simple page for table lookup and drilldown operations. Now, let's walk through the page wizard process once again and create a card page for a table. For this example, we will create a new table, **Contract Payment Terms**. In this table, the application will store payment terms that can be assigned to a contract—in particular, payment periods.

The following is the structure of the **50503 Contract Payment Terms** table:

Field no.	Field name	Data type	Length
1	Payment Terms Code	Code	20
2	Description	Text	50
3	Payment Date Formula	DateFormula	

The **Payment Terms Code** field is the table's primary key; **Description** is simply a text briefly describing the terms. **Payment Date Formula** is a **DateFormula** field, which we will use to calculate the next payment date.

To create a card page for the new table, open the object designer, switch it to page view, and choose the **File | New** option from the main menu. When in the **Page** view, this action runs the **New Page** dialog, which will suggest you choose between manual page creation and a page wizard.

Select the **Create a page using a wizard** option and **Card** as the page type, as follows:

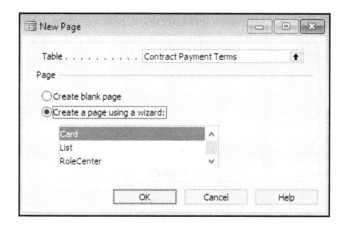

Selecting a wizard for a new page

After you push **OK**, the wizard shows the next page where you can add FastTab controls to the page, to organize controls in logical groups split into different tabs. **Contract Payment Terms** is a pretty simple table, and there is no need to divide its UI controls into groups. Leave the default **General** FastTab and press **Next**. The wizard will take you to the next page, where you can select the table fields that are to be shown in the page.

Fields can be reordered here; they will appear on the page in accordance with the order they are placed in the **Field Order** pane. Move all of the table fields from the left pane to the right and press **Next,** as follows:

Selecting fields for the page

The next wizard dialog allows you to insert subpages into you page. We will do this a little later, but for now just push **Finish** to skip this dialog and save the new page the **50502 Contract Payment Terms Card** page.

List pages

In the previous chapter, we already touched on the topic of creating card pages associated with a table. Now, let's take a closer look at the difference between card and list pages. Most entities in Dynamics NAV, such as customer, vendor, item, location, and so on, have at least two pages linked to the corresponding table. One of the pages represents one entity at a time, with all the details. This is a card page. The second one presents many records in tabular form, displaying only the most essential information. This form of presenting the table data is called a list page.

In the next example, we will create a list page for the **Customer Payment Terms** table to highlight the difference between card and list page types as follows:

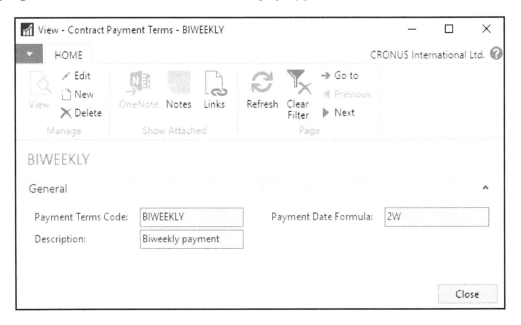

Card page

Basically, creating a list page is no different from what we just did for the card page type. These actions will lead you through the creation of a list page:

- Create a new page and choose **Create a page using a wizard** and **List** for the page type.
- In the **Table** text box, select the **50503 Contract Payment Terms** table.
- Push **OK** and select all table fields in the next wizard step.
- Press **Finish** and save the object as **50503** or **Contract Payment Terms List.**

The new page is shown in this screenshot:

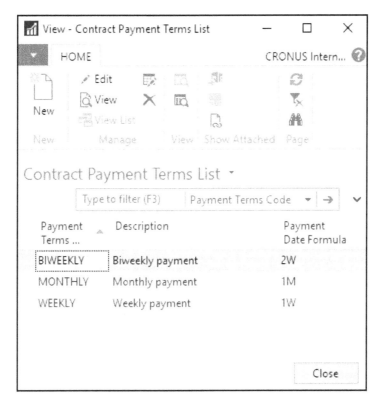

List page

ListPart and CardPart pages – subpages and FactBoxes

Dynamics NAV gives us many examples of advanced pages where some kind of subpage is embedded into a main page, offering additional information related to the entity being viewed. Different documents are always based on this principle: the main document page displays the document header, while various types of subpages represent document lines and detail the entities related to the document, such as customer, vendor, item, fixed asses, and so on.

In the next section, we will create a document page presenting the lease contract, and add contract lines in a subpage. In a separate subpage, we will report the current payment balance to the customer.

ListPart subpage

ListPart is a type of subpage that displays records in a list and synchronizes its output with the container page; its usual application is a list of document lines. ListPart built into a document page displays the lines of the document that is currently open in the main page. Now, we will create a page for the contract with a linked subpage for contract lines.

First of all, to embed a subpage into a container, we must have a container page itself. The the steps described in the previous section create a card page for the **50500 Lease Contract Header** table. Not all of the table fields are required on the page. In the page creation wizard, include the following fields in the page design:

- **No.**
- **Customer No.**
- **Starting Date**
- **Ending Date**
- **Total Amount**
- **Amount Paid**

This is going to be a **50505 Lease Contract** page, a document page for the contract, and a container for two subpages. The first of the subpages included in the document will display the document lines.

Create a page using a wizard, and select **ListPart** from the list of page types and **50501 Lease Contract Line** table, for the page source table.

Primary key fields in a **Subpage** representing document lines are usually hidden, since these values are filled automatically by the NAV platform, and users don't need to pay special attention to them. Therefore, the fields that should be displayed on the **Subpage** are **Item No.**, **Description**, and **Amount**. Choose these fields in the page creation wizard, press **Finish**, and save the new page as **50504 Lease Contract Subform**. We give it a name ending with **Subform** thanks to an old NAV tradition. Almost all of the subpages that you can see in the page designer have a name ending with **Subform** instead of **Subpage**, because most of these objects were created when the page object did not exist and the UI was presented in forms. To keep the naming consistent, new subpages are still dubbed Subforms.

The last field in the primary key of the **Lease Contract Line** table is a **Line No.** integer. It is usual to set up automatic assignment of the line number for subpage representing document lines. To make the number assigned when a new line is created, we need to enable the **AutoSplitKey** property for the **Lease Contract Subform** page. Access the design of the page, and in the page properties set the value of the **AutoSplitKey** property to **Yes**. With **AutoSplitKey** enabled, whenever a new line is inserted in the page, it will receive a number the same way as normally happens with other documents, such as purchase or sales orders, invoices, service orders, and so on.

For the **AutoSplitKey** property to assign new line numbers correctly, the page must satisfy two conditions:

- Records in the page must be sorted by the primary key.
- The data type of the last field in the primary field must be one of these types: **Integer**, **BigInteger**, **GUID**, or **Decimal**.

After saving the subpage, open the **Lease Contract** document page in the designer and insert a control, as shown in the screenshot:

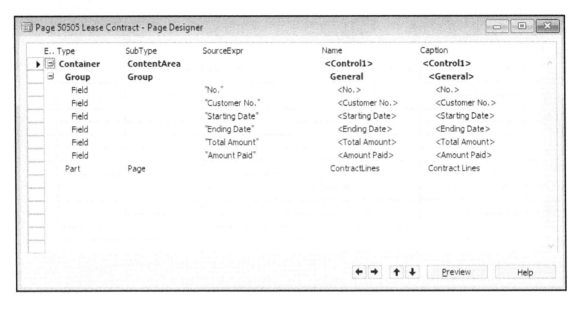

Adding a ListPart subpage to a document page

The type of the new control should be **Part**, and the SubType **Page**. Note the alignment of page design elements. A new page part must be indented on the same level as the **General** group. Use arrow buttons below the list of page elements to adjust indentation.

When the lines part is aligned in the page designer, open its properties and locate the **PagePartID** property. In this property, we specify the page object that will be shown as a subpage. Enter the 50504 page ID or its name, Lease Contract Subform.

To complete the subpage setup, we must set up a property, **SubPageLink,** which controls the subpage's recordset. The assist button in the property value field opens a link editor window. Fill in the link fields as in the following table:

Field	Type	Value
Contract No.	FIELD	No.

After confirming the link setup, the value of the **SubPageLink** property is `Contract No.=FIELD(No.)`. You can see the configured page part in this screenshot:

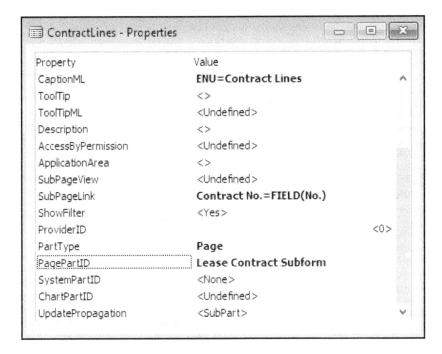

ListPart page properties

One more thing to do after completing the document page is update the contract list page created earlier. To add view and edit buttons that will lead to the document page from the list, we must set the **CardPageID** property. Open the **50500 Lease Contracts** page, in the page designer, navigate to its properties, and set the **CardPageID** property to the ID **50505** document page or its name, **Lease Contract**.

FactBox subpages

FactBox subpages are typically used to present some additional information related to the main entity shown on the page. Usually, information that does not directly affect the order, but is nice to know, is placed here. For example, when you create a sales order, a customer FactBox contains information about the current customer balance, available credit limit, and contact details. Another FactBox will detail item availability in the selected location.

In our demo application, we will create a FactBox page displaying the total amount summarized by all customer orders, and a total payments amount for the same customer. Follow these steps to create a FactBox page:

- Start by creating a new page in the page designer, the same as for a normal page.
- Specify the customer table as the source table for the page.
- Create a page using a wizard and choose the **CardPart** page type.
- In the next wizard dialog, you will be asked to add fields to your new page. Do not add any fields, just press **Finish**. Since both fields we want to include in the view are calculated dynamically, we will add them to the page manually.
- Save the object as page **50506, Lease Contract Customer Stats.**

The new page we just created consists of a single **ContentArea** container named **<Control1>**. The name is not critical, but it's always recommended to give meaningful names to page controls. Rename the container from **<Control1>** to **CustomerStats** and change the caption to **Customer Statistics**.

The next step in creating the **FactBox** page is declaring global variables, which will be used for calculating customer balances. Declare the following variables in C/AL Globals:

Name	Data type
TotalContracts	Decimal
TotalPayments	Decimal

The values of these variables must be calculated on the page. For this purpose, we will create a function: `CalculateCustomerTotals`. Declare this function in page 50506, C/AL Globals. The function code is in this code block:

```
LOCAL PROCEDURE CalculateCustomerTotals(
  VAR TotalCustomerContracts : Decimal;
  VAR TotalCustomerPayments : Decimal;CustomerNo : Code[20]);
VAR
  LeaseContractHeader : Record 50500;
BEGIN
  LeaseContractHeader.SETRANGE("Customer No.",CustomerNo);
  IF LeaseContractHeader.FINDSET THEN
    REPEAT
      LeaseContractHeader.CALCFIELDS("Total Amount","Amount Paid");
      TotalCustomerContracts += LeaseContractHeader."Total Amount";
      TotalCustomerPayments += LeaseContractHeader."Amount Paid";
    UNTIL LeaseContractHeader.NEXT = 0;
END;
```

The previous function summarizes the total contract amount from all the customer contracts in a variable, **TotalCustomerContracts**, and all amounts paid by the customer in the **TotalCustomerPayments** variable. Now, when we have the desired values calculated, we need page controls to show the values. To create a page control, follow these simple steps:

1. Close the C/AL editor to return to the page layout designer and add a new line, then choose **Field** as the control type.
2. In the **SourceExpr** field, click the assist button and select the **TotalContract** from the Symbols menu.
3. Change the name of the control to **TotalContractsControl**, change caption to **Total Contracts**.
4. This control should not be editable, so access its properties and set the value of the editable property to FALSE.

Then, following the same steps, create one more control in the page designer. This control will show the value of the **TotalPayments** global variable. The final page layout should look like the following screenshot:

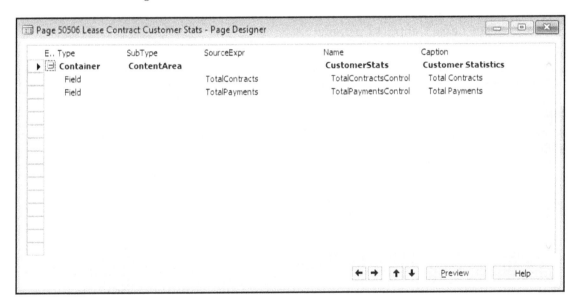

FactBox fields

Now, we will assign values calculated by the `CalculateCustomerTotals` function to page controls. The calculation should be called from the `OnAfterGetCurrRecord` page trigger. Open the C/AL editor, locate the trigger, and add the calling code, which is given as follows:

```
OnAfterGetCurrRecord()
    CalculateCustomerTotals(TotalContracts,TotalPayments,"No.");
```

The FactBox subpage has been completed now, and the last thing left to do is to insert it into its container page. This FactBox is a part of the **Lease Contract** page. The following short walk-through shows how to insert a subpage into a container and establish a link:

1. Open the **50505 Lease Contract** page, in the page designer.
2. Add a line to the page layout. Select the **Container** type, and a SubType of **FactBoxArea**.
3. Add another line under the **FactBoxArea** container. Type = **Part**, SubType = **Page**. Note the indentation of both container and page part controls. The correct indentation is shown in the following screenshot.
4. Select the last line in the designer (page part control) and open its properties. In the **PagePartID** property, specify the ID or the name of the FactBox subpage: **50506 Lease Contract Customer Stats**.
5. In the **SubPageLink** property line, click the assist button and construct the link formula: `No.=FIELD(Customer No.)`. This is done the same way as we did for the page lines Subform.

Finally, the completely designed contract page contains one page part for the lines, and another page part in a separate container for the FactBox. The structure of page controls is shown in this screenshot:

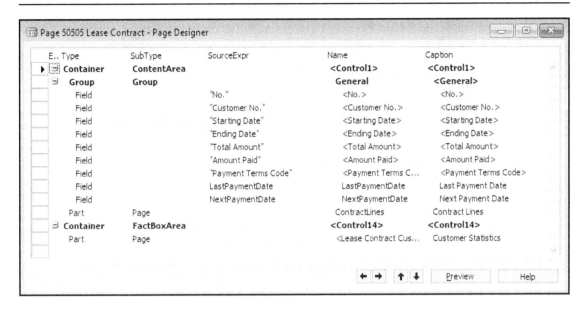

Design of a page with subpage and FactBox

When the page is run, the **Contract Lines** subpage is under the **General** tab, and the FactBox is moved from the main page content area. The next screenshot illustrates the same page when it is opened in the NAV client:

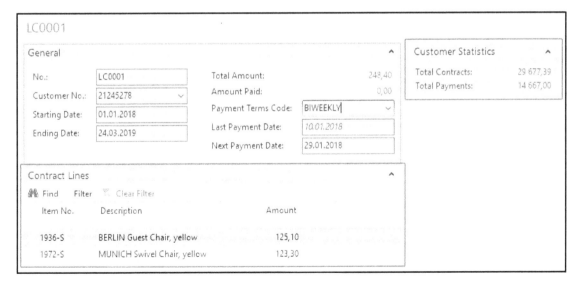

Document page with lines and a FactBox

The **Payment Terms Code**, **Last Payment Date,** and **Next Payment Date** controls in the previous two screenshots have not been described yet. To display values in these fields, we need to run C/AL code in page triggers. This is explained in the following section.

Page triggers – C/AL code in pages

Most of C/SIDE objects can contain C/AL triggers which are executed in response to different user actions, and pages are not exception. In this section, we will familiarize ourselves with most common page triggers, their practical values, and their limitations.

For the next code example, we will need to extend the **Lease Contract Header** table. In the **Card and List pages** section, we created a table representing different types of contract payment schedules. Now, this table must be linked to the contract. To do this, open **50500 Lease Contract Header** table, in the table designer and add a field as follows:

Field no.	Field name	Data type	Length
9	Payment Terms Code	Code	20

After declaring the field in the table, access its properties, and enter a new value for the **TableRelation** property. It should be **Contract Payment Terms**. Don't forget the quotation marks; a value without these will be rejected as an incorrect table name.

The new field must also be inserted into the **50505 Lease Contract** card page, which was created in the previous section. Save the table, open the page in the designer, insert a control in the page layout, and specify the **Payment Terms Code** field in the **SourceExpr** property.

Also, two global variables in the **50505 Lease Contract** page, will be required to store the calculated dates:

Name	Data type
LastPaymentDate	Date
NextPaymentDate	Date

To find the date of the last payment related to a contract, we must filter the **Customer Payment** table by the **Contract No.**, sort the result by the payment date, and select the last record. This will be done in a function that we will place in a new helper codeunit. Exit the page designer, create a codeunit **50504 Customer Payments Mgt.**, and declare a global function in the **FindLastCustomerPaymentDate** codeunit, as shown in the following code block:

```
PROCEDURE FindLastCustomerPaymentDate(ContractNo : Code[20]) : Date;
VAR
  CustomerPayment : Record 50502;
BEGIN
  CustomerPayment.SETCURRENTKEY("Contract No.","Payment Date");
  CustomerPayment.SETRANGE("Contract No.",ContractNo);
  IF CustomerPayment.FINDLAST THEN
    EXIT(CustomerPayment."Payment Date");

  EXIT(0D);
END;
```

When a new function is declared in the C/AL editor, its scope is local by default. To change it to global, open the function properties and change the value of the **Local** property to **No**.

In the same codeunit, create another function, `CalcNextPaymentDate`. Given a date and a contract number, this function will return the next expected payment date. The code of the function is in the next code block:

```
PROCEDURE CalcNextPaymentDate(ContractNo : Code[20];AtDate : Date) : Date;
VAR
  LeaseContractHeader : Record 50500;
  ContractPaymentTerms : Record 50503;
  PaymentDate : Date;
  I : Integer;
BEGIN
  LeaseContractHeader.GET(ContractNo);
  IF AtDate > LeaseContractHeader."Ending Date" THEN
    EXIT(0D);

  IF NOT ContractPaymentTerms.GET(LeaseContractHeader."Payment Terms Code")
THEN
    EXIT(0D);
  PaymentDate := LeaseContractHeader."Starting Date";
  WHILE (PaymentDate <= LeaseContractHeader."Ending Date") AND (PaymentDate
<= AtDate) DO
    PaymentDate := CALCDATE(ContractPaymentTerms."Payment Date
Formula",PaymentDate);

  IF PaymentDate > LeaseContractHeader."Ending Date" THEN
```

```
        PaymentDate := LeaseContractHeader."Ending Date";

    EXIT(PaymentDate);
END;
```

Open the **50505 Lease Contract** page, in the page designer and add a global variable:

Name	Data type	Subtype
CustomerPaymentsMgt.	Codeunit	Customer Payments Mgt.

Navigate to the C/AL code editor (**View | C/AL Code**). In the C/AL editor, access the global declarations and create a function, UpdatePaymentDates:

```
LOCAL PROCEDURE UpdatePaymentDates();
BEGIN
  LastPaymentDate :=
CustomerPaymentsMgt.FindLastCustomerPaymentDate("No.");
  NextPaymentDate :=
CustomerPaymentsMgt.CalcNextPaymentDate("No.",WORKDATE);
END;
```

Navigate to the OnAfterGetCurrRecord page trigger and modify it as follows:

```
OnAfterGetCurrRecord()
  UpdatePaymentDates;
```

Now, we have the last payment date and the next expected payment date calculated. The OnAfterGetCurrRecord page trigger fires every time a new record is read from the database and displayed in the page. And here, we recalculate dates each time the page data is updated.

Now, let's see how to use page triggers to dynamically modify the text format in page controls. What we want to do now is highlight contracts with overdue payments by changing the text color to red. We will make use of the same OnAfterGetCurrRecord trigger, to identify contracts that were not paid on time and apply an alternative text format to those contracts that have overdue payments.

The first thing to do is declare a global variable in the same page, **50505 Lease Contract**. Create a variable, OverduePayment : Boolean.

The function calculating the value will be called from the page, but it should be placed in the **50504 Customer Payments Mgt** codeunit. The function code is as follows:

```
PROCEDURE IsOverduePayment(ContractNo : Code[20]) : Boolean;
VAR
  PrevScheduledDate : Date;
```

```
    NextScheduledDate : Date;
    LastPaymentDate : Date;
BEGIN
    PrevScheduledDate := CalcPrevPaymentDate(ContractNo,WORKDATE);
    NextScheduledDate := CalcNextPaymentDate(ContractNo,WORKDATE);
    LastPaymentDate := FindLastCustomerPaymentDate(ContractNo);
    EXIT(NOT ((LastPaymentDate > PrevScheduledDate) AND (LastPaymentDate <=
NextScheduledDate)));
END;
```

Add one more line to the `UpdatePaymentDates` function to calculate the value of the new variable:

```
IsOverdue := CustomerPaymentsMgt.IsOverduePayment("Lease Contract
Header"."No.");
```

We have calculated the indicator telling us if the payment on the current contract was not paid on time. Now, we can use it to highlight the contract line and draw attention to it. Here is how you can change the style of a page control:

- In the table designer, select the **LastPaymentDate** field and open its properties
- For the property **Style**, select the **Attention** value
- In the **StyleExpr** property, enter the name of the **OverduePayment** variable

As a result of this setup, every time the value of the Boolean variable specified in the **StyleExpr** property is evaluated to **TRUE**, the **Attention** style will be applied to the **LastPaymentDate** control.

The same function, `UpdatePaymentDates`, must be called on validation of the **Starting Date**, **Ending Date**, and **Payment Terms Code** fields. Modification of any of these fields changes the payment schedule and will affect the next expected payment date and the contract's overdue status. Select the **LastPaymentDate** field and open the C/AL editor from this field (**View | C/AL Code**). The code editor will automatically focus on the triggers of the selected field. Add the function call in the `Starting Date — OnValidate` trigger. The next code block shows the code of the trigger:

```
Starting Date - OnValidate()
    UpdatePaymentDates;
```

Then, do the same for `Ending Date—OnValidate` and `Payment Terms Code—OnValidate`.

The OnValidate trigger in a page field will be called after OnValidate of the corresponding table field. For the Starting Date field, which now has trigger code in both the table and trigger, the OnValidate trigger in the **Lease Contract Header** table will fire first, followed by OnValidate in the **Lease Contract** page.

Lookups and DrillDowns

Now, we will implement drilldown functionality for the dynamically calculated fields of the contract's FactBox. The first thing to do is create list pages for contract lines and customer payments. These pages will support drilldown functionality for the total contract amount, and total paid amount, respectively. The first of these—**50500 Lease Contracts** page—was already described in the previous Chapter 3, *Tables - Creating Data Structure*.

Following walk-through will create a list page for payments:

1. Create a new page in the **Page Designer**, choose to use a wizard, then select the option **List** as a page type.
2. Select the **50502 Customer Payment** table, as the source table for the page.
3. In the first screen of the **List Page wizard**, include all table fields, except **Entry No.**, in the page.
4. Push **Finish**, then save the page, and assign the ID **50507** and the name **Customer Payments**.
5. Now, switch the object designer to the table view and open the design of the **50502 Customer Payment** table.
6. In the table properties, fill the values for the **LookupPageID** and **DrillDownPageID** properties. Set the page ID to **50507** for both.

Save the table. This will enable the drilldown functionality for the **CalcField** is **Amount Paid** in the **Lease Contract Header** table, which has a calculation formula. But, we still have to implement the OnDrillDown triggers for total payments and total contract amounts in the customer statistics FactBox.

Both the `DrillDownTotalPayments` and `DrillDownTotalContracts` functions should be declared in the **50506 Lease Contract Customer Stats** page. The first of these functions is in the next code block:

```
LOCAL PROCEDURE DrillDownTotalPayments(CustomerNo : Code[20]);
VAR
  CustomerPayment@1001 : Record 50502;
  CustomerPayments@1002 : Page 50507;
BEGIN
  CustomerPayment.FILTERGROUP(2);
  CustomerPayment.SETRANGE("Customer No.",CustomerNo);
  CustomerPayment.FILTERGROUP(0);

  CustomerPayments.SETTABLEVIEW(CustomerPayment);
  CustomerPayments.LOOKUPMODE(TRUE);
  CustomerPayments.EDITABLE(FALSE);
  CustomerPayments.RUN;
END;
```

The first of the statistics DrillDown functions opens a list of customer payments. All we need to do to show this list is filter the **Customer Payment** table by the customer code and assign the table view to the **Customer Payments** DrillDown page. The customer filter is applied in the *group 2* filter, then the active filter group is switched back to *group 0*, which is a group for user filters. This way, the filter on **Customer No.** will not be available for the user and cannot be removed manually.

The second function, `DrillDownTotalContracts`, which opens a list of contract lines, is a bit more tricky. We cannot directly apply a filter on contract lines, since the **Lease Contract Line** table does not have a customer reference; the customer code is only stored in the **Lease Contract Header** table. To collect the list of lines, a filter on **Customer No.** is applied on the header table, then the function loops through filtered contracts, collecting the lines of each contract into a buffer table. A function, `DrillDownTotalContracts`, shown in the following code block, should be created in the same page, **50506 Lease Contract Customer Stats**:

```
LOCAL PROCEDURE DrillDownTotalContracts(CustomerNo : Code[20]);
VAR
  LeaseContractHeader : Record 50500;
  LeaseContractLine : Record 50501;
  TempLeaseContractLine : TEMPORARY Record 50501;
BEGIN
  LeaseContractHeader.SETRANGE("Customer No.",CustomerNo);
  IF LeaseContractHeader.FINDSET THEN
  REPEAT
    LeaseContractLine.SETRANGE("Contract No.",LeaseContractHeader."No.");
    IF LeaseContractLine.FINDSET THEN
```

```
      REPEAT
        TempLeaseContractLine := LeaseContractLine;
        TempLeaseContractLine.INSERT;
      UNTIL LeaseContractLine.NEXT = 0;
    UNTIL LeaseContractHeader.NEXT = 0;

  PAGE.RUN(0,TempLeaseContractLine);
END;
```

Note the `TempLeaseContractLine` variable in the following code block. It is declared as a temporary table. To make a record variable refer to a temporary table instead of a normal database table, declare a `Record` type variable in the function, then open its properties, and select **Yes** for the temporary property.

No data manipulations performed on a temporary record are saved to the database. Records inserted into it are available as long as the variable remains in scope.

The last thing left to make DrillDowns work is to add function calls to the corresponding page triggers. In the **Lease Contract Customer Stats** page, add the following code to the `TotalContractsControl: OnDrillDown` trigger:

```
DrillDownTotalContracts("No.");
```

Then, call the second `DrillDown` function from `TotalPaymentsControl - OnDrillDown`:

```
DrillDownTotalPayments("No.");
```

Page action designer

Besides displaying table data in different formats, Dynamics NAV pages enable C/AL developers to extend functionality by creating action buttons that execute C/AL code when pushed. As an example of the page action, we will augment the contract page with an action creating sales invoices based on the payment schedule. For simplicity, we will not store the whole payment schedule and invoice history, but will note only the date of the last invoice. To keep this date, a new field in the **Lease Contract Header** table is required. So, before continuing with the action, open **50500 Lease Contract Header** table, in the table designer and add a field, **Last Invoice Date**, as per this table:

Field no.	Field name	Data type
10	Last Invoice Date	Date

This is going to be an internal field, used in the code, so we will not show it in the page.

Now, save the table and open codeunit **50504 Customer Payments Mgt.,** in the object designer.

In the C/AL Globals declaration of the codeunit, create a new global function, CreateSalesInvoiceHeader, as follows:

```
PROCEDURE CreateSalesInvoiceHeader(VAR SalesHeader : Record 36;VAR
LeaseContractHeader : Record 50500);
VAR
  ContractPaymentTerms : Record 50503;
BEGIN
  IF NOT ContractPaymentTerms.GET(LeaseContractHeader."Payment Terms Code")
THEN
    ERROR(MissingPayTermsErr);

  SalesHeader.VALIDATE("Document Type",SalesHeader."Document
Type"::Invoice);
  SalesHeader.VALIDATE("Sell-to Customer No.",LeaseContractHeader."Customer
No.");

  IF LeaseContractHeader."Last Invoice Date" = 0D THEN
    SalesHeader.VALIDATE("Document Date",LeaseContractHeader."Starting
Date")
  ELSE
    SalesHeader.VALIDATE(
      "Document Date",CALCDATE(ContractPaymentTerms."Payment Date Formula",
      LeaseContractHeader."Last Invoice Date"));
  SalesHeader.VALIDATE("Posting Date",SalesHeader."Document Date");
  SalesHeader.INSERT(TRUE);

  LeaseContractHeader.VALIDATE("Last Invoice Date",SalesHeader."Document
Date");
  LeaseContractHeader.MODIFY(TRUE);
END;
```

This function creates an invoice header based on the contract data. The text constant used in the code should be declared in C/AL Globals as follows:

```
MissingPayTermsErr: TextConst 'ENU=To create an invoice, fill the payment
terms code.'
```

Another function, CreateSalesInvoiceLines, should be declared in the same codeunit. This is a function that will create invoice lines corresponding to lease contract lines, and it is shown in the following code block:

```
PROCEDURE CreateSalesInvoiceLines(SalesHeader : Record 36;ContractNo :
Code[20]);
VAR
  SalesLine : Record 37;
  LeaseContractLine : Record 50501;
  LineNo : Integer;
BEGIN
  LeaseContractLine.SETRANGE("Contract No.",ContractNo);
  IF LeaseContractLine.FINDSET THEN
    REPEAT
      LineNo += 10000;
      SalesLine.INIT;
      SalesLine.VALIDATE("Document Type",SalesHeader."Document Type");
      SalesLine.VALIDATE("Document No.",SalesHeader."No.");
      SalesLine.VALIDATE("Line No.",LineNo);
      SalesLine.VALIDATE(Type,SalesLine.Type::Item);
      SalesLine.VALIDATE("No.",LeaseContractLine."Item No.");
      SalesLine.VALIDATE(Quantity,1);
      SalesLine.VALIDATE("Line Amount",LeaseContractLine.Amount);
      SalesLine.INSERT(TRUE);
    UNTIL LeaseContractLine.NEXT = 0;
END;
```

A third function in the same codeunit, **50504 Customer Payments Mgt.,** will wrap the creation of the invoice header and lines into one function call.

The CreateSalesInvoice function, creates an invoice header by calling CreateSalesInvoiceHeader, then passes the document header received from it to the next function, CreateSalesInvoiceLines. See the following function code:

```
PROCEDURE CreateSalesInvoice(VAR LeaseContractHeader : Record 50500);
VAR
  SalesHeader@1001 : Record 36;
BEGIN
  CreateSalesInvoiceHeader(SalesHeader,LeaseContractHeader);
  CreateSalesInvoiceLines(SalesHeader,LeaseContractHeader."No.");
END;
```

This is the function that will be invoked from our new action button. To execute a code triggered when a user presses an action button, this code must be placed in the button's `OnAction` trigger. But first, the action itself must be created in the page action designer. Here are the steps describing how to add a new action:

1. Open **50505 Lease Contract** page, in the **Page Designer**.
2. Navigate to the **Page Action Designer** (**View ⏐ Page Actions**, or *Ctrl + Alt + F4*).
3. A new action container is inserted with the default subtype, **NewDocumentItems**. Change the subtype to **ActionItems**.
4. Add a name and a caption to the action container. Enter **Documents** for both properties.
5. Add another line with the type **Action**. Assign a name, **CreateInvoice**, and a caption, **Create Invoice**.
6. Select the action line in the designer and open the **Properties** window (**View ⏐ Properties**).
7. Here, change two button properties. Set **Promoted = Yes** and **PromotedCategory = Process**.
8. Do not leave properties yet. In the same window, find the **Image** property and choose the image named **CreateDocument** from the list of available images:

Page action designer

After the action is inserted, it is time to add trigger code that will be run when the action is activated. Select the last action line and open the C/AL code editor. In the `OnAction` trigger, declare a local variable that will refer to the **Customer Payments Mgt.** codeunit and simply call the `CreateSalesInvoice` function with the current record as a parameter, as in the following code snippet:

```
OnAction=VAR
  CustomerPaymentsMgt : Codeunit 50504;
BEGIN
  CustomerPaymentsMgt.CreateSalesInvoice(Rec);
END;
```

This completes the design of the action button. Run the **Lease Contract** page in the NAV client to review the results. The next screenshot shows the page with the action just created:

Action button in Windows client

The **ActionItems** action container places the button in a separate tab on the page, **ACTIONS**. Also, since we created it as **Promoted**, the action will be duplicated in the **Process** category in the **HOME** tab.

Menu suite

In all code examples in this book so far, whenever we wanted to execute an object, we just ran it directly from the object designer. While this method works perfectly fine for an application developer, this is apparently not the way users are supposed to open pages and execute actions. Objects executed from the user interface must be arranged in the user menu with MenuSuite objects.

User menu design has a layered structure; several menu suites can exist in the system, each one consolidating a set of objects on its own menu design level. The basic application menu structure provided by Microsoft is described in the MenuSuite object 1010, **Dept - MBS**. Any localized version of NAV also includes a country-level menu in the **Dept - Country** menu suite, and in some cases a region-level **Dept - Region**.

Up to ten add-on menus can co-exist in one application; these are developed by ISV partners who provide add-on solutions. Customized menus are typically created at the **Partner** and **Company** design levels.

To create your custom application menu, switch the object designer to the MenuSuite view and choose **File** | **New action**. To create a MenuSuite object, you must choose the menu design level. Design level selection is shown in this screenshot:

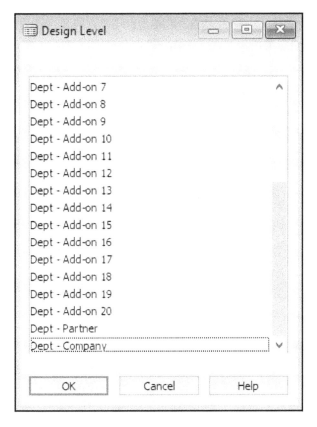

Menu design levels

If you are a Microsoft partner, select the **Dept - Partner** level. The **Dept - Company** option is for a customer with the developer's license. The **OK** button in the **Design Level** window will bring you to the menu designer. To create a new menu in the selected design level, right-click in the menu area and choose the **Create Menu...** option from the drop-down menu, as shown here:

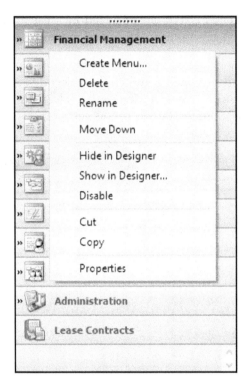

Create Menu

In the next dialog, you can define the menu caption and choose a bitmap. Enter **Lease Contracts** for the caption.

As for the bitmap, there is no list of bitmaps to choose from inside NAV. You'll have to Google it if you want an overview, or just fiddle with the setup. This property only accepts a number from 0 to 15, so there are 16 predefined menu images to select from.

When the menu is created, you can build its structure by filling the menu with groups and items. Select the new menu in the application menu area. Its name will be displayed in the designer header line as **Dept - Company: Lease Contracts**. The first part depends on the design level selected earlier: **Dept - Company** for the company-level menu and **Dept - Partner** for the partner level.

Now, the menu contains a single entry marked as **[Empty Menu]**. Right-click on the caption and choose **Create Group**. By default, the group just created receives a name, **New Group**. Rename it **Contracts**. This way, you define a menu group, a submenu that does not lead to an object, but that presents another level of the menu structure.

Right-click on the **Contracts** group and choose the **Create Item** option shown in the following screenshot:

Creating a menu item

Menu item is the lower level of the menu structure. Menu items contain references to C/SIDE objects that must be executed when the menu item is selected. It is possible to create menu items in the main menu, skipping the group level, as well as create nested menu groups. If a menu consists of three or four items, probably there is no need to split it into groups. On the other hand, it would be difficult to find an item among a hundred others in one group. The choice of the appropriate structure is yours.

To complete the creation of a menu item, fill in its properties in the next dialog window. Here is a list of parameters to be set in the dialog:

1. Choose the **Page** option in the object type.
2. Enter the object ID that will be executed by this menu item: 50500. The page name **Lease Contracts** can be entered instead of the ID.
3. The caption will be set automatically from the object, but you can change it manually.
4. In the **Department** options, choose **Documents**:

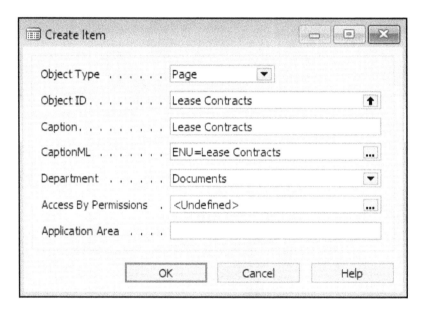

Menu item properties

Following the same steps, create another menu item for payment terms. Configure the new item to show the the page **50503 Contract Payment Terms List** in the **Tasks** department. Close the menu designer and confirm the request to save the changes.

Start the Dynamics NAV role-tailored client (or close and reopen it if it was started). Your shiny new application menu should be as shown in the following screenshot:

MenuSuite in the NAV Windows client

Now, we can run all C/SIDE objects from the menu created here.

Summary

In this chapter, we developed a user interface for the add-on module started in previous chapters. After completing the exercises, you can create simple pages with a page wizard, and construct a more complex presentation layer including document subpages and FactBoxes. Besides, now you know how to customize the functionality of UI elements with C/AL code, and can build a well-structured user menu.

The next chapter is dedicated to data exchange. We will familiarize ourselves with a new object type, XMLPort, and walk through developing a data exchange interface with an external system.

Exchanging Data with XML Ports

5

It is hard to imagine a corporate information system that does not exchange data with external databases. Bank payments and reconciliation statements, tax reports, application configuration—information goes in and out of the system. Data exchange can be implemented in different formats, but the *de facto* standard of data exchange is XML, which also has native support in NAV.

C/SIDE offers a special type of object for importing and exporting XML data: XMLport. Besides XML, XMLports can transfer data in simple delimiter-separated format, **comma-separated values** (**CSV**), or **delimiter-separated values** (**DSV**). Throughout this chapter, we will be developing objects for data exchange in different formats. The chapter will cover the following topics:

- Importing data from CSV files
- Importing data from XML files
- XMLport triggers
- Exporting table data
- Designing the request page
- Running XMLports from C/AL code

Importing data from CSV files

CSV is the simplest way of presenting structured data. It is a text file where each line represents a table record, and record fields are separated with a comma—hence the name CSV. The data file is very compact: it does not carry any markup data except field delimiters, and the format is easily mapped to relational databases where tables are native data storage.

Although a comma is the default field separator in NAV XMLports, it is actually defined by object properties and can be changed, which turns the file into a DSV instead of a native CSV. Now, we will create an XMLport for importing customer payment data from an external text file with a semicolon as a field delimiter.

In the next example, we need to extend the customer payment table and add new fields to it, as follows:

Field No.	Field Name	Data Type	Length
7	Journal Line Posted	Boolean	
12	Customer No.	Code	20
13	Corrected	Boolean	
14	Bank Account No.	Code	20

Now, we have all the fields we need to create an XMLport and load data into the table. Create an XMLport in the object designer and save it with the ID and name **50500 Import Customer Payments CSV**:

Node Name	Node Type	Source Type	Data Source
root	Element	Text	
CustomerPayment	Element	Table	\<Customer Payment\>(Customer Payment)
ContractNo	Element	Field	Customer Payment::Contract No.
ContractLineNo	Element	Field	Customer Payment::Contract Line No.
PaymentDate	Element	Field	Customer Payment::Payment Date
Amount	Element	Field	Customer Payment::Amount
DepartmentCode	Element	Field	Customer Payment::Global Dimension 1 Code
ProjectCode	Element	Field	Customer Payment::Global Dimension 2 Code
CustomerGroupCode	Element	Field	Customer Payment::Customer Group Code
SalesPersonCode	Element	Field	Customer Payment::Salesperson Code
CustomerNo	Element	Field	Customer Payment::Customer No.
BankAccountNo	Element	Field	Customer Payment::Bank Account No.

When designing the structure of the XMLport, pay attention to the line indentation in the **Node Name** column. The base element of the structure must be a **Text** element, and the table being exported comes as a child node for the root. The root element is not actually exported and does not appear in the resulting CSV file. The **Table** element must be indented under the root, and all **Field** elements come under the table with further indentation. To align data elements, use the arrow buttons at the bottom of the page. The **XMLport Designer** is shown in the following screenshot:

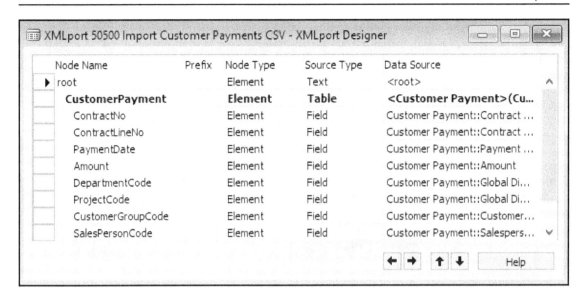

XMLport Designer

We want to import data from a variable-text CSV file with a semicolon as a field separator. The same applies for data export, as the XMLport we are developing for CSV format supports exporting as well. All export parameters are defined in the object properties. To access the XMLport properties, select the empty line under the bottom element in the editor and select the **View** | **Properties** menu action. When positioned on a data element line, the same action will open the properties of the selected element instead.

The first key property for us is **Format**. It defines the format of the output file: variable text, fixed text, or XML. By default, a new XMLport is created in XML format. Change this value to **Variable Text** to export data into a CSV file with a delimiter.

After selecting the variable text format, you can also choose delimiters that will separate values in a data stream:

- `FieldDelimiter`: The symbol that will mark the beginning and ending of each field. Leave the default quotation mark.
- `FieldSeparator`: A value placed between two fields in a record. Change the default comma to semicolon (;).

- `RecordSeparator`: Symbol separating records within one table. The default is a **<<NewLine>>**, which is fine for us. This means that every new line in the file begins a separate table record.
- `TableSeparator`: This is how you want to separate tables if data from several tables is combined in one file. The default value is a double new line (**<<NewLine><NewLine>>**), but we are not going to mix tables in this example, so it does not matter.

As you can see, the configuration created in the XMLport does not include the **Entry No.** field, which is the primary key for the **Customer Payment** table. This is an internal value specific to the NAV data structure and is not coded in the external data file. To assign a value to the entry number, we can use C/AL code (and we will do this a little later). But it is not mandatory to initialize the entry number in C/AL triggers; this task could be delegated to SQL Server. To make the server assign the primary key value automatically when the record is inserted, perform the following actions:

1. Open table **50502 Customer Payment** in the table designer.
2. Select the **Entry No.** field and navigate to **Properties** (**View** | **Properties**).
3. Choose the **AutoIncrement** property and change its value to **Yes**.

With this setup, the value of the primary key field **Entry No.** will be incremented automatically when a new record is inserted.

A sample data structure for importing is shown in the next block. If you run a data export with the same XMLport, you will receive a file with exactly the same fields:

```
"LC0001";"10000";"10.01.18";"186,00";"ADM";"VW";"MEDIUM";"JR";"21245278"
"LC0001";"20000";"10.01.18";"258,00";"ADM";"TOYOTA";"INSTITUTION";"JR";"212
45278"
"LC0002";"10000";"10.01.18";"1587,00";"PROD";"VW";"LARGE";"MD";"01905893"
"LC0003";"10000";"10.01.18";"2637,00";"SALES";"VW";"MEDIUM";"MD";"21245278"
"LC0003";"20000";"10.01.18";"235,00";"SALES";"MERCEDES";"PRIVATE";"MD";"212
45278"
"LC0003";"30000";"10.01.18";"9764,00";"SALES";"TOYOTA";"LARGE";"MD";"212452
78"
```

Now, the setup is in place to import payment information from a CSV file. Just run the XMLport from the object designer and select a file to import when requested.

Importing data from XML files

The XML format was developed as a flexible and human-readable standard for data exchange. It allows us to define complex hierarchical structures, which can include a schema for data validation. But a significant drawback of this format is its verbosity and the volume of auxiliary markup data.

It is not designed for the presentation of relational data; rather for a representation of objects.

The hierarchical nature of XML allows us to group payments by bank account. In the next section, we will use this structure in data exporting.

In an XMLport representing an XML document, a root element is also mandatory. But unlike in the CSV case, this root element is exported; this is the root XML node. **BankAccount** is the child of the root node **Payments**, and this is mapped to a text element instead of a table field, as we did in the CSV example. A bank account is used to group underlying payment records. Create an XMLport in the object designer and save the new object with the ID and name **50501 Import Customer Payments XML**. The data structure of the XMLport is in next table:

Node Name	Node Type	Source Type	Data Source
Payments	Element	Text	<Payments>
BankAccount	Element	Text	<BankAccount>
AccountNo	Attribute	Text	BankAccountNo
CustomerPayment	Element	Table	<Customer Payment>(Customer Payment)
ContractNo	Element	Field	Customer Payment::Contract No.
ContractLineNo	Element	Field	Customer Payment::Contract Line No.
PaymentDate	Element	Field	Customer Payment::Payment Date
Amount	Element	Field	Customer Payment::Amount
DepartmentCode	Element	Field	Customer Payment::Global Dimension 1 Code
ProjectCode	Element	Field	Customer Payment::Global Dimension 2 Code
CustomerGroupCode	Element	Field	Customer Payment::Customer Group Code
SalesPersonCode	Element	Field	Customer Payment::Salesperson Code
CustomerNo	Element	Field	Customer Payment::Customer No.

A fragment of the XML structure generated by this XMLport is shown as follows:

```
<Payments>
  <BankAccount AccountNo="NBL">
    <CustomerPayment>
      <ContractNo>LC0002</ContractNo>
      <ContractLineNo>10000</ContractLineNo>
      <PaymentDate>10.01.18</PaymentDate>
      <Amount>1 587,00</Amount>
      <DepartmentCode>PROD</DepartmentCode>
      <ProjectCode>VW</ProjectCode>
      <CustomerGroupCode>LARGE</CustomerGroupCode>
      <SalesPersonCode>MD</SalesPersonCode>
      <CustomerNo>01905893</CustomerNo>
    </CustomerPayment>
  </BankAccount>
</Payments>
```

For this code to work, we need two new fields in the **Lease Contract Setup** table. The fields are described as follows:

Field No.	Field Name	Data Type	Length
4	Cust. Payment Jnl. Template	Code	10
5	Cust. Payment Jnl. Batch	Code	10

After declaring the table field, set up table relations. This is straightforward for the **Cust. Payment Jnl. Template** field: just open the field's properties and select the **Gen. Journal Template** table in the **TableRelation**.

For the second field, **Cust. Payment Jnl. Batch**, it is more complicated, since its reference depends on the value selected in the **Cust. Payment Jnl. Template** field. To set up the table relationship with a filter, follow these steps:

1. Open the **Properties** window for the **Cust. Payment Jnl. Template** field.
2. In the **TableRelation** property, push **AssistButton** to open the table relation setup.
3. In the **Table field**, select **Gen. Journal Batch**.
4. In the **Field** field, select **Name**.
5. In **Table Filter**, press the **AssistButton**, this time to open the table filter setup.
6. In **Field**, select **Journal Template Name**.
7. In the **Type**, choose **FIELD**.
8. In the **Value** field, select the table **Cust. Payment Jnl. Template** field.

Push **OK** in all open setup windows. In the end, the final filter should be this:

```
"Gen. Journal Batch".Name WHERE (Journal Template Name=FIELD(Cust. Payment
Jnl. Template))
```

This rather complicated setup sequence means that now the list of journal batches shown in the lookup page will depend on the selected journal template. Every journal batch has a template it belongs to, and batch names in the list will be filtered by the template name, which is selected in the **Cust. Payment Jnl. Template** field.

When new fields are configured in the table, add these to the setup page **50508 Lease Contract Setup**. To modify the page, open it in the page designer and add fields to the page layout, as per the following table:

Type	SourceExpr	Name	Caption
Field	Cust. Payment Jnl. Template	<Cust. Payment Jnl. Template>	<Cust. Payment Jnl. Template>
Field	Cust. Payment Jnl. Template	<Cust. Payment Jnl. Template>	<Cust. Payment Jnl. Template>

For this setup, you only need to select **Field** as the element type in each line, and select the source field in the **C/AL Symbol** menu. The name and caption are automatically copied from the selected field.

This step completes the configuration of the XMLport structure, but to make it work we still have amend it with C/AL code. Unlike the CSV file in the previous example, the XML structure developed here is hierarchical, with the bank account being a parent element to all payments made via the same account. This structure cannot be matched to a table and needs some additional processing logic. The next section explains how to implement this logic in XMLport C/AL triggers.

XMLport triggers

As with most other C/SIDE objects, XMLports provide a set of triggers that can be customized with C/AL code. Most of these triggers are related to import and export events and provide the possibility to control the data flow in the middle of its migration from an external source to NAV tables, or vice versa.

This section will give you an overview of the most important and frequently used XMLport triggers, with some suggestions on how to use these triggers in your application.

Earlier in this chapter, we configured the primary key field of the **Customer Payment** table to receive new values automatically upon inserting a record. This approach slightly simplifies application code, but it has its drawback: it does not allow the NAV server to use a performance optimization known as buffered insert. With the **Allow Buffered Insert** option enabled, the NAV server can combine several records into a single SQL INSERT query. When many records are inserted sequentially, this optimization reduces the number of database queries. But with the **AutoIncrement** option on a table field, each record must be inserted separately and the optimization cannot be used.

In the next example, we will disable **AutoIncrement**, allowing the NAV server to benefit from the buffered insert option.

To control the number of the entry to be inserted, declare a global variable in the EntryNo : Integer XMLport.

The variable just declared will be used in the OnPreXMLport trigger, which fires when the object is initialized, but before it starts processing data. In the case of data imports, this trigger is executed before reading the file. When exporting, it precedes reading any tables that take part in the export procedure.

We will use this trigger to initialize the EntryNo variable, keeping the number of the next payment entry to be inserted in the table. The following line of code should be inserted in the OnPreXMLport trigger:

```
OnPreXMLport()
  EntryNo := FindNextPaymentEntryNo;
```

The following is the FindNextPaymentEntryNo function, which returns the number to be assigned to the next payment entry:

```
LOCAL PROCEDURE FindNextPaymentEntryNo() : Integer;
VAR
  CustomerPayment : Record 50502;
BEGIN
  IF CustomerPayment.FINDLAST THEN
    EXIT(CustomerPayment."Entry No." + 1);

  EXIT(1);
END;
```

`OnBeforeInsertRecord` fires when the data is read from the imported file and the record is initialized and about to be inserted into the database table. It serves the purpose of filling in the fields that are not directly imported from the external file, but must be filled in by internal system logic. This is also the place where you can verify the correctness of the imported data. If you use XML format for data exchange, XMLport validates imported data against the XML schema when the file is read. Any other checks that go beyond simple schema validation can be implemented in the `OnBeforeInsertRecord` trigger.

In this example, we will use the trigger to set the value of **Entry No.** and increment the global counter. The processing logic for imported payment entries is also implemented here.

If the imported payment already exists in **Customer Payments**, it is considered a corrective entry and its further processing depends on the current status of the payment, whether the corresponding journal lines were already created and posted or not:

```
Customer Payment - Import::OnBeforeInsertRecord=BEGIN
  "Customer Payment"."Bank Account No." := BankAccountNo;
  "Customer Payment"."Entry No." := EntryNo;

  MakeCorrectionIfPaymentExists(
    "Customer Payment"."Contract No.",
    "Customer Payment"."Contract Line No.",
    "Customer Payment"."Payment Date");

  EntryNo += 1;
END;
```

The `MakeCorrectionIfPaymentExists` function is called in the previous code snippet and is detailed in the following code. Before inserting the new payment record, we analyze if the same payment already exists and how to handle it in the case of a repeated import. Action in this case will depend on the status of the previously imported payment, whether the payment journal line was already created for the same payment, and whether it was posted:

```
LOCAL PROCEDURE MakeCorrectionIfPaymentExists(
  ContractNo : Code[20];ContractLineNo : Integer;PaymentDate : Date);
VAR
  CustomerPayment : Record 50502;
BEGIN
  IF
FindCustomerPayment(CustomerPayment,ContractNo,ContractLineNo,PaymentDate)
THEN
    IF CustomerPayment."Journal Line Created" THEN
      IF CustomerPayment."Journal Line Posted" THEN
        InsertCorrectivePaymentEntry(CustomerPayment)
```

```
        ELSE BEGIN
          DeletePaymentJournalLine(CustomerPayment);
          SetPaymentCorrectionMark(CustomerPayment);
        END
      ELSE
        SetPaymentCorrectionMark(CustomerPayment);
    END;
```

Deeper in the callstack, we check whether the payment exists. The `FindCustomerPayment` function shown next uses the `FINDLAST` statement to look for a payment line with matching parameters, which is not marked as corrected. When a corrective payment record is imported, the existing one receives a correction mark:

```
LOCAL PROCEDURE FindCustomerPayment(
  VAR CustomerPayment : Record 50502;
  ContractNo : Code[20];
  ContractLineNo : Integer;
  PaymentDate : Date) : Boolean;
BEGIN
  CustomerPayment.SETRANGE("Contract No.",ContractNo);
  CustomerPayment.SETRANGE("Contract Line No.",ContractLineNo);
  CustomerPayment.SETRANGE("Payment Date",PaymentDate);
  CustomerPayment.SETRANGE(Corrected,FALSE);
  EXIT(CustomerPayment.FINDLAST);
END;
```

When a payment journal line is already created from a customer payment record (but not posted yet), we delete the journal line. This is done in the following `DeletePaymentJournalLine` function:

```
LOCAL PROCEDURE DeletePaymentJournalLine(VAR CustomerPayment : Record
50502);
VAR
  GenJournalLine : Record 81;
  CustPaymentGenJnlLine : Record 50504;
BEGIN
  IF CustPaymentGenJnlLine.GET(CustomerPayment."Entry No.") THEN
    IF GenJournalLine.GET(
      CustPaymentGenJnlLine."Gen. Jnl. Template Name",
      CustPaymentGenJnlLine."Gen. Jnl. Batch Name",
      CustPaymentGenJnlLine."Gen. Jnl Line No.")
    THEN
      GenJournalLine.DELETE(TRUE);
END;
```

The earlier imported payment record is not deleted when a correction is imported. Instead, we mark the old record as `Corrected` and insert a correction line. Two functions in the next code block perform this function. `SetPaymentCorrectionMark` will set the correction mark, while the second function, `InsertCorrectivePaymentEntry`, creates a copy of the initial entry, changing the sign of the amount:

```
LOCAL PROCEDURE SetPaymentCorrectionMark(VAR CustomerPayment : Record
50502);
BEGIN
  CustomerPayment.VALIDATE(Corrected,TRUE);
  CustomerPayment.MODIFY(TRUE);
END;

LOCAL PROCEDURE InsertCorrectivePaymentEntry(CustomerPayment : Record
50502);
VAR
  CorrCustomerPayment : Record 50502;
BEGIN
  CorrCustomerPayment := CustomerPayment;
  CorrCustomerPayment.VALIDATE("Entry No.",EntryNo);
  CorrCustomerPayment.VALIDATE(Amount,-CustomerPayment.Amount);
  CorrCustomerPayment.INSERT(TRUE);
  EntryNo += 1;
END;
```

When customer payment data is imported, payment records must be converted to payment journal lines to post the lines and have all information logged in financial registers. The following is the `CreatePaymentJournalLines` function, which will do the processing. The function should be declared in the management codeunit **50504 Customer Payments Mgt.**, but it is going to be called from an action trigger on the **Customer Payments** page . Create an action button on page 50507, then declare this function and invoke it from the button's `OnAction` trigger:

```
PROCEDURE CreatePaymentJournalLines(VAR CustomerPaymentFilter : Record
50502);
VAR
  CustomerPayment : Record 50502;
BEGIN
  CustomerPayment.COPYFILTERS(CustomerPaymentFilter);
  CustomerPayment.SETRANGE("Journal Line Created",FALSE);
  IF CustomerPayment.FINDSET THEN
    REPEAT
      CreatePaymentJournalLine(CustomerPayment);
    UNTIL CustomerPayment.NEXT = 0;
  CustomerPayment.MODIFYALL("Journal Line Created",TRUE);
END;
```

The following function is the one where the two fields added to the **Lease Contract Setup** table earlier in this chapter will be required. `CreatePaymentJournalLine` inserts a record into the **Gen. Journal Line** table, and codes of journal template and journal batch are taken from the setup table. Also, the journal template setup provides a number series for the internal document number:

```
LOCAL PROCEDURE CreatePaymentJournalLine(CustomerPayment1 : Record 50502);
VAR
  LeaseContractSetup : Record 50505;
  GenJournalLine : Record 81;
  BankAccount : Record 270;
  GenJournalTemplate : Record 80;
  NoSeriesManagement : Codeunit 396;
BEGIN
  LeaseContractSetup.GET;
  WITH GenJournalLine DO BEGIN
    VALIDATE("Journal Template Name",LeaseContractSetup."Cust. Payment Jnl.
Template");
    VALIDATE("Journal Batch Name",LeaseContractSetup."Cust. Payment Jnl.
Batch");
    SETRANGE("Journal Template Name",LeaseContractSetup."Cust. Payment Jnl.
Template");
    SETRANGE("Journal Batch Name",LeaseContractSetup."Cust. Payment Jnl.
Batch");
    IF FINDLAST THEN;
    "Line No." += 10000;
    GenJournalTemplate.GET("Journal Template Name");
    BankAccount.GET(CustomerPayment."Bank Account No.");
    VALIDATE("Posting Date",CustomerPayment."Payment Date");
    VALIDATE("Document Type","Document Type"::Payment);
    VALIDATE(
      "Document No.",
      NoSeriesManagement.GetNextNo(GenJournalTemplate."No. Series","Posting
Date",TRUE));
    VALIDATE("Account Type","Account Type"::Customer);
    VALIDATE("Account No.",CustomerPayment."Customer No.");
    VALIDATE("Bal. Account Type","Bal. Account Type"::"Bank Account");
    VALIDATE("Bal. Account No.",CustomerPayment."Bank Account No.");
    VALIDATE("Currency Code",BankAccount."Currency Code");
    VALIDATE(Amount,CustomerPayment.Amount);
    INSERT(TRUE);
  END;
END;
```

Exporting table data

A simple XMLport, where each data element is mapped to a table field, can be used to transfer data in both directions: export from a table to a file, or import into a table. If a data file has a more complex structure, bidirectional transfer may not be possible. An XMLport can be configured for import, export, or both operations if you intend to combine both import and export in a single object.

The supported direction of data transfer is defined by the **Direction** property, which receives the default value **Both** in a new XMLport. If left unchanged, this option enables the user to choose the direction upon execution of the object. When an XMLport developed for both import and export is run, an option, **Direction**, is available in the request page, as shown in this screenshot:

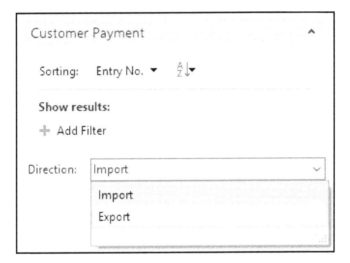

Direction option

When the **Direction** is selected in the object properties, it is fixed and users cannot change it at runtime.

To export customer payments, we will create a modified copy of the **50501 Import Customer Payments XML** XMLport, but will change it slightly to adapt the object for exporting data instead of importing. The following table shows a part of the XMLport containing the modified element. In the original XMLport, **50501 Import Customer Payments XML**, the **BankAccount** and **AccountNo** elements are both text variables that are processed:

Node Name	Node Type	Source Type	Data Source
Payments	Element	Text	<Payments>
BankAccount	Element	Table	<Bank Account>(Bank Account)
AccountNo	Attribute	Field	Bank Account::No.
CustomerPayment	Element	Table	<Customer Payment>(Customer Payment)

This dataport will only export data. We are not going to use it for import, and this means that the **Direction** option should be hidden from the request page. To remove the option, access the XMLport properties and select the **Direction** property . Possible values for this property are **Import**, **Export**, or **Both**, with **Both** being the default value. When this option is selected, this means that the object supports import as well as export, and the user can choose themselves. If the data flow direction is fixed to import or export only, the selection will not be shown on running the XMLport. For the current use case, choose **Export** for the **Direction** property.

Select the **BankAccount** data item and add the following code in its trigger, `Bank Account – Export::OnAfterGetRecord`:

```
Export::OnAfterGetRecord=VAR
  CustomerPayment : Record 50502;
BEGIN
  CustomerPayment.SETRANGE("Bank Account No.","Bank Account"."No.");
  IF CustomerPayment.ISEMPTY THEN
    currXMLport.SKIP;
END;
```

The `OnAfterGetRecord` trigger is executed each time a record is retrieved from the table, and before this record is exported. And here, we can perform additional processing of records before sending them to export. The preceding code sample employs the trigger to run a check on each bank account. If a bank account does not have any related payments, the `currXMLport.SKIP` function is called. The `currXMLport` variable is similar to `CurrPage` for page objects. Like `CurrPage`, it is a system variable that exists in any XMLport objects and always refers to the current object itself. Calling SKIP on the XMLport makes it skip the processing of the current record, thus excluding it from the export. This way, the preceding code will exclude from the export any bank accounts without linked customer payments.

Designing the request page

It is not necessary to export all data from tables included in the XMLport structure. When the object is executed, a request page provides an interface to filter records and narrow down the dataset being exported. This is one of the examples of using the XMLport request page. Any other options the developer wants to suggest to users could be placed on the request page.

Technically, a request page is a page object not much different from normal pages discussed in `Chapter 4`, *Designing User Interface*. This kind of page is created via the same designer with a content area container, control groups, and controls, and includes the same set of triggers. The main difference is that a request page is a part of an XMLport or a report object and cannot be executed separately from its host object.

We will discuss reports and report request pages in the next chapter. Now, let's design a custom request page for an XMLport.

The next table describes the structure of a new XMLport that will be used in the request page demo. Create the XMLport object and assign it the ID and name **50508 Export Lease Contracts**:

Node Name	Node Type	Source Type	Data Source
LeaseContracts	Element	Text	<LeaseContracts>
Contract	Element	Table	<Lease Contract Header>(Lease Contract Header)
No	Element	Field	Lease Contract Header::No.
CustomerNo	Element	Field	Lease Contract Header::Customer No.
StartingDate	Element	Field	Lease Contract Header::Starting Date
EndingDate	Element	Field	Lease Contract Header::Ending Date
ContractLine	Element	Table	<Lease Contract Line>(Lease Contract Line)
LineNo	Element	Field	Lease Contract Line::Line No.
ItemNo	Element	Field	Lease Contract Line::Item No.
Description	Element	Field	Lease Contract Line::Description
Amount	Element	Field	Lease Contract Line::Amount

When the XMLport structure is defined, set up the table link between two elements: **Contract** and **ContractLine**. To configure the table link, select the **ContractLine** element and set the linking properties as follows:

- LinkTable: Lease Contract Header
- LinkFields: Contract No.=FIELD(No.)

There is one more important bit of setup to do in the data item properties. We want to enable users to filter exported records at the contract level, but don't want them to filter separate contract lines. To disable user filters on a data item, a **SourceTableView** property must be configured in the designer. The value of the property does not matter. It's simple: if the property is not blank, filtering fields for this data item will be excluded from the request page.

So, to exclude filters on the **ContractLine** data item, it is enough to select a sorting order for lines. To select sorting, follow these steps:

- Push **AssistButton** in the property value to open the table view setup.
- In the **Key** field, select the only available key, **Contract No.,Line No.**
- Press **OK** to confirm the selection.

When the table view is configured, the **SourceTableView** property is changed to **SORTING(Contract No.,Line No.)**.

If you expect your users to filter data on FlowFields, add the respective fields to the list of autocalculated values in the data item. XMLport exporting contract data is based on the **Lease Contract Header** table, which has two FlowFields: **Total Amount** and **Amount Paid**. To enable filtering on these two fields, select the data item corresponding to the table (the one with the node name **Contract**) and open its properties. Press the **AssistButton** for the property **CalcFields** and select the two FlowFields. Now, the values of these fields will be automatically calculated when the next record is retrieved from the table, and it will be possible to apply filters on the fields.

Updating FlowFields on each record can slow down data export significantly. Enable autocalculation only when necessary.

So far, we have discussed how to enable or disable system-created filtering fields. Now, let's look at an additional custom filter and apply it to the exported record set. This will include an option to enable or disable exporting completely paid contracts.

Execute the **View | Request Page** menu action. This command opens the request page designer, which is not unlike the usual page designer. To create a request page, you will need a container and fields, which can be combined in control groups inside the container. The screenshot illustrates the page designer with the setup required for the request page:

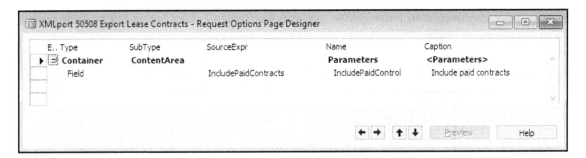

XMLport request page designer

The global variable that is going to be bound to the page control.
`IncludePaidContracts: Boolean`. The value of the variable should be initialized on startup. By default, we want to export all contracts, so the value will be set to TRUE. Add the following code in the `OnInitXMLport` trigger:

```
OnInitXMLport()
  IncludePaidContracts := TRUE;
```

The `OnInitXMLport` trigger is executed before any other code in the object, and this is a good place to initialize global variables. Now, let's add the code that will analyze the user input and skip contracts when necessary. The following code should be placed in the `Lease Contract Header: Export::OnAfterGetRecord` trigger:

```
Export::OnAfterGetRecord=BEGIN
  IF NOT IncludePaidContracts THEN BEGIN
    "Lease Contract Header".CALCFIELDS("Total Amount","Amount Paid");
    IF "Lease Contract Header"."Amount Paid" >= "Lease Contract
Header"."Total Amount" THEN
        currXMLport.SKIP;
  END;
END;
```

As in the previous section, where we skipped bank accounts without customer payments, here we use the `OnAfterGetRecord` trigger to exclude certain records from export. If the `IncludePaymentContracts` checkbox is unchecked and the contract is paid in full, the `currXMLport.SKIP` function is called and the current contract record is not exported.

 The same function, SKIP, can be called when records are imported. If it is called in the trigger `Lease Contract Header: Import::OnBeforeInsertRecord`, the record being processed will not be imported.

Finally, save the object and run it. Now, you can see the new checkbox in the request page, as follows:

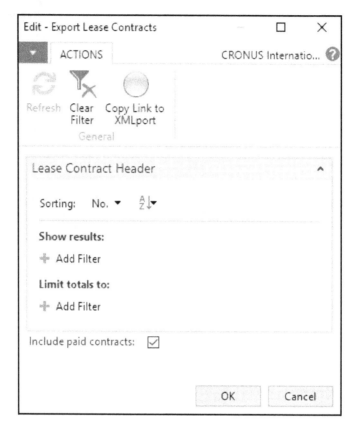

Customized XMLport request page

Running XMLports from C/AL code

Although an XMLport can be called from a user menu and present its own request page to set up parameter, often it proves useful to invoke the import or export routine directly from the application code. This provides more flexibility to the object functionality and allows the developer to control data exchange at a deeper level.

For example, running an XMLport as a C/AL variable allows you to do the following:

- Replace the standard file open dialog with a different one, or exclude it and generate a filename without requiring the user to enter it
- Set predefined filters on data items and control table records being imported or exported
- Import from and export to any Stream object, not necessarily a file stream

Exporting data from a C/AL function

The next code example demonstrates how to use this feature. We will call the **Export Lease Contracts** XMLport from a page to export the selected contract, without opening the request page.

The `ExportContract` function shown in the code block exports the contract record by directing the XMLport output into a file stream. The `SETTABLEVIEW` function is used to limit the export to records satisfying the filtering criteria applied to the `LeaseContractHeader` variable. Before calling `SETTABLEVIEW`, we set a filter on the contract number to select a single record; in practice it, can be any viable table filter. This function should be declared on page **50505 Lease Contract**, and will be called on the same page:

```
LOCAL PROCEDURE ExportContract(ContractNo : Code[20]) : Boolean;
VAR
  LeaseContractHeader : Record 50500;
  FileManagement : Codeunit 419;
  ExportLeaseContracts : XMLport 50508;
  FileStream : OutStream;
  FileName : Text;
  OutFile : File;
BEGIN
  FileName := FileManagement.SaveFileDialog('Export
contract','','xml|*.xml');
  IF FileName = '' THEN
    ERROR('');

  IF EXISTS(FileName) THEN
    ERASE(FileName);

  OutFile.CREATE(FileName);
  OutFile.CREATEOUTSTREAM(FileStream);

  LeaseContractHeader.SETRANGE("No.",ContractNo);
  ExportLeaseContracts.SETTABLEVIEW(LeaseContractHeader);
```

```
    ExportLeaseContracts.SETDESTINATION(FileStream);
    EXIT(ExportLeaseContracts.EXPORT);
  END;
```

To receive the filename, the function opens a dialog, `SaveFileDialog`. If the selected file already exists, it is deleted and recreated again. We don't ask the user to confirm the overwriting of the file, since this confirmation request is raised by the `SaveFileDialog` function in **File Management**. The dialog will not return the filename if the user selects an existing file and then does not confirm the choice.

To break function execution when the user cancels the action, we use a little trick: we call the `ERROR` function with the empty string in the parameter. The `ERROR('')` syntax will stop the function execution silently, without showing any error messages.

To invoke the export function, create an action button on page **50505 Lease Contract**. There is already an action container, **Documents**, on this page, which we created in `Chapter 4`, *Designing User Interface*. New actions can be added to the same container. Create the action with the parameters shown in the following table:

Type	Name	Caption
Action	ExportContract	Export Contract

This action will require two global text constants:

Name	ConstValue
ContractExportedMsg	Contract was successfully exported
CouldNotWriteFileErr	Could not write file

The `OnAction` trigger of the action button we just created calls the `ExportContract` function and displays a message, depending on the export status, as shown in the next code block:

```
OnAction=BEGIN
  IF ExportContract("No.") THEN
    MESSAGE(ContractExportedMsg)
  ELSE
    MESSAGE(CouldNotWriteFileErr);
END;
```

With the new action, you can run the XML export, hiding the native XMLport interface and controlling its functionality from your C/AL function. The resulting code is more complicated than the simple `XMLport.RUN`, but it gives you detailed control over object execution.

Importing XML from C/AL

Importing data via XMLport directly from C/AL code is very similar to exporting. The `ImportPayments` function, which is listed in the next block, mostly performs the same actions as `ExportContract`, discussed previously. At the beginning of the function, we identify the filename from which records will be imported. Unlike the previous example, in this case there is obviously no code to overwrite an existing file; we only need to read it. If the file does not exist, the import will fail. Table filtering and `SETTABLEVIEW` are also not needed here. We only need an `InStream` object to link the XMLport with the input file and to call the `IMPORT` function:

```
LOCAL PROCEDURE ImportPayments() : Boolean;
VAR
  FileManagement : Codeunit 419;
  ImportCustomerPayments : XMLport 50501;
  FileStream : InStream;
  InFile : File;
  FileName : Text;
BEGIN
  FileName := FileManagement.OpenFileDialog('Import customer
payments','','xml|*.xml');
  IF FileName = '' THEN
    ERROR('');

  InFile.OPEN(FileName);
  InFile.CREATEINSTREAM(FileStream);

  ImportCustomerPayments.SETSOURCE(FileStream);
  EXIT(ImportCustomerPayments.IMPORT);
END;
```

Similar to the previous example, this code will be called from a page action. Create an action button on the **Customer Payments** page. There is already an action container with an action, **Create Journal Lines**, so just add another action to it, assigning properties as follows:

Type	Name	Caption
Action	ImportPayments	Import payments

To display a text message after competing the import, declare two text constants in the page:

Name	ConstValue
PaymentsImportedMsg	Payments imported successfully
ImportFailedErr	Could not import file

The action button simply calls the function and shows a message, depending on the result received:

```
OnAction=BEGIN
  IF ImportPayments THEN
    MESSAGE(PaymentsImportedMsg)
  ELSE
    MESSAGE(ImportFailedErr);
END;
```

Summary

In this chapter, we exchanged data with external data sources, received customer payment information, and sent payments back in XML and CSV formats. With simple examples, the chapter explained how to design an XMLport without any coding and how to create more intricate export and import procedures in the C/AL language.

The next chapter will lead you through the designing of report objects, from the simplest table presentation to complex calculations involving temporary tables to store intermediate results.

6
NAV Event Model

In the previous chapters, we developed new C/SIDE objects and placed code in our own custom functions. But very often, it happens that the developer needs to change base NAV application code. You probably added a new field to a ledger table and want to fill it in when a journal line is posted, or you need to show additional dialog when an action button is pressed on the **Sales Order** page.

But it is not always possible to modify objects included in the base application; license restrictions may prevent you from editing these objects. And even if your license allows modifications, it is recommended that you avoid them if possible for a simple reason. Any cumulative update released by Microsoft can be simply imported into your database if application objects are not modified. If base objects have custom modifications, applying official hot fixes to them may become a much more complicated task.

Different types of application events help customize functionality without modifying objects. By subscribing to events, you can hook your handlers to user actions, database triggers, or key points of business scenarios, and execute your own code, avoiding intrusion into base objects.

In this chapter, you will learn how to handle different types of events and publish your own events. The chapter covers the following topics:

- Integration events
- Database events
- UI events
- Publishing custom events
- Manual event subscription

Integration events

As was mentioned in the introductory paragraph of this chapter, events may be raised by various processes in NAV. Here are some examples of events:

- Database trigger events are raised when table records are inserted, deleted, or updated.
- Page trigger (UI) events are initiated by the platform on UI actions such as validation of a page field, activation of an action button, page opening and closing, and so on.
- Business and integration events are raised explicitly by C/AL code. These events correspond to certain logical points in the application, and are defined by application developers. This type of event can be raised by C/AL developers, as we will see later in this chapter.

Now, we begin with a discussion of an event model of the last type: business and integration events. Both types are combined under one header, because basically, there is no difference between them from the implementation point of view. The only distinction between business and integration event types is in the considerations behind each event. A business event is considered a part of the system API that cannot be changed in future releases, whereas integration events do not carry these assumptions, although, technically speaking, no restrictions are imposed on the modification of any event.

Both business and integration events are a special type of C/AL procedure that is invoked by the application code. Both types are bound to application logic and triggered at some points in the process, where external code could fit in to extend functionality.

For example, in the general journal posting routine, such logical points include checking the batch balance, posting the journal batch, checking each line, and posting each line. Every step in the process raises one or more events, as follows:

- OnBeforeCheckBalance
- OnBeforeCheckAccountNo
- OnAfterCheckGenJnlLine
- OnBeforeStartPosting
- OnAfterPostGLAcc

This is only a small portion of the long list of events triggered during journal posting—key points where you can inject your own logic into the posting routine.

To illustrate the subscription to integration events, we will hook our handler to the sales posting routine in order to update a contract record when an invoice created from the same record is posted.

To refer to the created invoice and mark the contract when the invoice is posted, we will extend the **50500 Lease Contract Header** table. New fields must be created in the table, as follows:

Field No.	Field Name	Data Type	Length
11	Invoice No.	Code	20
12	Invoice Posted	Boolean	

The data model described for the lease contracts in `Chapter 3`, *Tables – Creating Data Structure*, does not allow us to match an invoice with the contract it was initiated from. To fix this, we are introducing the **Invoice No.** field, which must be filled in when the invoice record is inserted. The invoice is created by the `CreateSalesInvoice` function in codeunit **50504 Customer Payments Mgt.**. Modify its code as shown in the next code block:

```
IF LeaseContractHeader."Invoice No." = '' THEN
  EXIT;

CreateSalesInvoiceHeader(SalesHeader,LeaseContractHeader);
CreateSalesInvoiceLines(SalesHeader,LeaseContractHeader."No.");

LeaseContractHeader.VALIDATE("Invoice No.",SalesHeader."No.");
LeaseContractHeader.MODIFY(TRUE);
```

Now, after creating a sales invoice, we have to link to it from the lease contract itself, and can update the linked contract once again when the invoice is posted. We will do this in an integration event handler that is going to be bound to one of the events triggered on sales document posting.

In the object designer, create a new codeunit; call it codeunit **50515 Lease Contract Events**. This is going to be the object responsible for handling events related to lease contracts.

In the codeunit, create a function, `UpdateContractOnPostInvoice`. Access the function properties and change the value of the **Event** property from the default **No** to **Subscriber**. When a function is declared as an event subscriber, the object designer will display more event-related properties that must be configured to subscribe to events. These properties include **EventPublisherObject** and **EventFunction**. The meaning of both properties is obvious: the first one is the ID of the object publishing the event we want to subscribe to, and the second property is the name of the event function. For **EventPublisherObject**, select **codeunit Sales-Post**. In the **EventFunction** field, select **OnAfterPostSalesDoc**.

The event subscriber inherits its signature from the publisher method, and the NAV dev environment updates it for you when you select the publisher. The code editor will ask you if you want to overwrite the signature of the function. Confirm the request and close the event subscriber properties. This is what the request looks like:

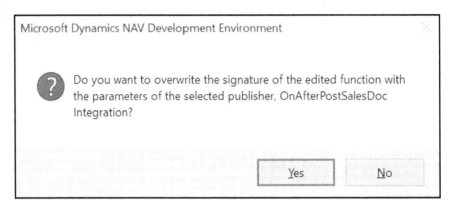

Request to overwrite function signature

After you confirm the request, the `UpdateContractOnPostInvoice` function will automatically receive a new signature, as shown in the following code block:

```
LOCAL [EventSubscriber] UpdateContractOnPostInvoice(
  VAR SalesHeader : Record "Sales Header";
  VAR GenJnlPostLine : Codeunit "Gen. Jnl.-Post Line";
  SalesShptHdrNo : Code[20];
  RetRcpHdrNo : Code[20];
  SalesInvHdrNo : Code[20];
  SalesCrMemoHdrNo : Code[20])
```

Now, return to the code editor and write the code of the event subscriber itself. The following code sample omits the list of function parameters, as it's already shown in the previous code block:

```
LOCAL PROCEDURE UpdateContractOnPostInvoice(...);
VAR
  LeaseContractHeader : Record 50500;
BEGIN
  IF SalesHeader."Document Type" <> SalesHeader."Document Type"::Invoice
THEN
    EXIT;
  WITH LeaseContractHeader DO BEGIN
    SETRANGE("Invoice No.",SalesHeader."No.");
    IF FINDFIRST THEN BEGIN
      VALIDATE("Invoice Posted",TRUE);
```

```
        MODIFY(TRUE);
      END;
    END;
  END;
```

Design **50500 Lease Contract Header** table, open the table keys (**View | Keys**), and create a key on the **Invoice No.** field. Since we are applying a filter on this field, a key will improve the performance of database queries.

As soon as you compile and save the codeunit containing the event subscriber, the subscription will be activated. The event handler will be executed every time a sales document is posted or, to be precise, when the `OnAfterPostSalesDoc` function of the **Sales-Post** codeunit, which we selected as the event source, is executed. Since it fires on the posting of any sales document, we need additional checks in the beginning to make sure that the document being posted is an invoice. If the document type is confirmed, we can search the related lease contract header that needs an update. The document that is being posted in the Sales-Post codeunit is passed to the event handler in the **SalesHeader** parameter.

Now, we want to perform a similar update for customer payments. The **Customer Payment** record is marked as posted when the user posts a related general journal line.

To store the relation between payment records and journal lines, we will create a new table, as follows:

Field No.	Field Name	Data Type	Length
1	Customer Payment Entry No.	Integer	
2	Gen. Jnl. Template Name	Code	10
3	Gen. Jnl. Batch Name	Code	10
4	Gen. Jnl. Line No.	Integer	

Save the table with the ID and name **50504 Cust. Payment - Gen. Jnl. Line**. Close it and reopen it again. Only now can you start configuring table relations. The table relation for the **Gen. Jnl. Batch Name** field uses a filter based on a value of another field, and this relation cannot be set up until all fields involved in the relation are saved in the metadata:

- **Customer Payment Entry No.**: Table relation for **Customer Payment**
- **Gen. Jnl. Template Name**: Table relation for the **Gen. Journal Template** table

Actually, these two relations can be configured without saving the table. It's the table relation of the **Gen. Jnl. Batch Name** field that requires the table to be saved. Configure the table relation for the "Gen. Journal Batch" field, or just copy the code from the next block to the **TableRelation** property:

```
"Gen. Journal Batch".Name WHERE (Journal Template Name=FIELD(Gen. Jnl.
Template Name))
```

Subscribe to the OnBeforePostGenJnlLine event of Codeunit 12. Place the subscriber function in codeunit **50515 Lease Contract Events**. The subscriber function code is in the next code block. It will capture the event of posting the general journal lines and update the related customer payment:

```
[EventSubscriber(Codeunit,12,OnBeforePostGenJnlLine)]
LOCAL PROCEDURE UpdateCustPaymentOnPostJournalLine(VAR GenJournalLine :
Record 81);
VAR
  CustPaymentGenJnlLine : Record 50504;
  CustomerPayment : Record 50502;
BEGIN
  IF GenJournalLine."Document Type" <> GenJournalLine."Document
Type"::Payment THEN
    EXIT;

  WITH CustPaymentGenJnlLine DO BEGIN
    SETRANGE("Gen. Jnl. Template Name",GenJournalLine."Journal Template
Name");
    SETRANGE("Gen. Jnl. Batch Name",GenJournalLine."Journal Batch Name");
    SETRANGE("Gen. Jnl. Line No.",GenJournalLine."Line No.");
    IF FINDFIRST THEN BEGIN
      CustomerPayment.GET("Customer Payment Entry No.");
      CustomerPayment.VALIDATE("Journal Line Posted",TRUE);
      CustomerPayment.MODIFY(TRUE);
    END;
  END;
END;
```

Event subscribers can be declared only in codeunits. Any C/SIDE object containing application code can publish events.

Database trigger events

Database trigger events are raised on data manipulations: when a record is being inserted, deleted, or updated. Each of these database events has two counterparts in C/AL: one event is raised before the data change occurs in the database, and the second one after data modification. The names of these events begin with `OnBefore` and `OnAfter`, respectively. There are eight events related to C/AL data manipulation functions:

- `OnBeforeInsertEvent`
- `OnAfterInsertEvent`
- `OnBeforeDeleteEvent`
- `OnAfterDeleteEvent`
- `OnBeforeModifyEvent`
- `OnAfterModifyEvent`
- `OnBeforeRenameEvent`
- `OnAfterRenameEvent`

Two other events, `OnBeforeValidateEvent` and `OnAfterValidateEvent`, are raised when a field is validated: before the field's `OnValidate` trigger is executed and after it is completed.

We will employ database triggers to keep control of invoices linked to lease contracts. When an invoice is created, we save its number in the `Lease Contract Header` table. But it is possible for the invoice to be deleted without posting. Then, the number kept in the contract will make no sense anymore and should be removed. Without events, the only way to update the linked table on deleting the invoice is to customize the `OnDelete` trigger of the **Sales Invoice Header** table. To avoid modifications of the base code, we can subscribe to a corresponding `OnAfterDeleteEvent`. To create a subscriber, declare a new function in codeunit **50515 Lease Contract Events**. Name it `UpdateContractOnDeleteInvoice` and update the following function properties:

- **Event**: `Subscriber`
- **EventPublisherObject**: `Table Sales Header`
- **EventFunction**: `OnAfterDeleteEvent`

The code of the function is as follows:

```
[EventSubscriber(Table,36,OnAfterDeleteEvent)]
LOCAL PROCEDURE UpdateContractOnDeleteInvoice(VAR Rec : Record
36;RunTrigger : Boolean);
VAR
```

```
      LeaseContractHeader : Record 50500;
   BEGIN
     IF Rec."Document Type" <> Rec."Document Type"::Invoice THEN
       EXIT;

     WITH LeaseContractHeader DO BEGIN
       SETRANGE("Invoice No.",Rec."No.");
       IF FINDFIRST THEN
         IF NOT "Invoice Posted" THEN BEGIN
           VALIDATE("Invoice No.",'');
           MODIFY(TRUE);
         END;
     END;
   END;
```

The event we just subscribed to is triggered every time a sales document is deleted. If the document being deleted is not an invoice, we can skip further processing and exit the function. For invoices, we check whether they are linked to any contract, and if the contract is found, the invoice reference is removed from it.

Note the `Rec` variable in the event subscriber parameters. As you know, tables and pages always have a global system variable, `Rec`, containing the current record. Database events also send the `Rec` variable to subscribers, but here it is not a system variable (which is not available in codeunits), simply a parameter name.

The same update is required for customer payment records when a payment journal line, created earlier, is deleted. In this case, the event to subscribe to is the same `OnAfterDeleteEvent` in table **81 Gen. Journal Line**. The event subscriber is a new function, `UpdateCustPaymentOnDeleteJnlLine`, in the codeunit **Lease Contract Events**. Set its properties as follows:

- **Event**: `Subscriber`
- **EventPublisherObject**: `Table Gen. Journal Line`
- **EventFunction**: `OnAfterDeleteEvent`

The function code is as follows. As for any other event subscriber, you don't have to declare function parameters manually; these are updated by the development environment to match the event publisher's signature:

```
[EventSubscriber(Table,81,OnAfterDeleteEvent)]
LOCAL PROCEDURE UpdateCustPaymentOnDeleteJnlLine(VAR Rec : Record
81;RunTrigger : Boolean);
VAR
  CustPaymentGenJnlLine : Record 50504;
  CustomerPayment : Record 50502;
```

```
BEGIN
  IF Rec."Document Type" <> Rec."Document Type"::Payment THEN
    EXIT;

  WITH CustPaymentGenJnlLine DO BEGIN
    SETRANGE("Gen. Jnl. Template Name",Rec."Journal Template Name");
    SETRANGE("Gen. Jnl. Batch Name",Rec."Journal Batch Name");
    SETRANGE("Gen. Jnl Line No.",Rec."Line No.");
    IF FINDFIRST THEN BEGIN
      CustomerPayment.GET("Customer Payment Entry No.");
      CustomerPayment.VALIDATE("Journal Line Created",FALSE);
      CustomerPayment.MODIFY(TRUE);

      DELETE(TRUE);
    END;
  END;
END;
```

The next example employs another database trigger event, `OnBeforeModifyEvent`, to block an attempt to modify the amount in a contract-related invoice. Again, a `BlockOnModifySalesLine` function should be created in the **Lease Contract Events** codeunit with the following properties:

- **Event**: `Subscriber`
- **EventPublisherObject**: `Table Sales Line`
- **EventFunction**: `OnBeforeModifyEvent`

Before coding the function, declare a global text constant, **ModifyNotAllowedErr**, in the **Lease Contract Events** codeunit. This constant will be used in the function code: `ModifyNotAllowedErr : TextConst 'ENU=Invoice %1 was created from the contract %2. Invoice amount cannot be modified'`.

As in the `OnAfterDeleteEvent`, `OnBeforeModifyEvent` subscriber receives a `Rec` variable which contains the modified record. But it also has a second parameter, `xRec`, which is a copy of the record as it was before the modification. This structure once again mimics tables and pages where the system `xRec` variable shows the record state before the modification took place in the `OnModify` table trigger. Hence, we can rely on the `Rec` and `xRec` variables to find out which fields were changed:

```
[EventSubscriber(Table,37,OnBeforeModifyEvent)]
LOCAL PROCEDURE BlockOnModifySalesLine(VAR Rec : Record 37;VAR xRec :
Record 37;RunTrigger : Boolean);
VAR
  LeaseContractHeader : Record 50500;
BEGIN
```

```
        IF (Rec."Document Type" <> Rec."Document Type"::Invoice) OR
           (Rec."Line Amount" = xRec."Line Amount")
        THEN
          EXIT;

        WITH LeaseContractHeader DO BEGIN
          SETRANGE("Invoice No.",Rec."No.");
          IF FINDFIRST THEN
            ERROR(ModifyNotAllowedErr,"Invoice No.","No.");
        END;
      END;
```

Here, we compare the Rec **Line Amount** with the xRec **Line Amount** to determine whether it has been modified, and if not, just leave the function, since we want to block only the modification of the amount, which must be aligned with the contract. When the error is thrown inside the OnBeforeModify event, the current transaction is rolled back and modifications are not saved to the database.

For general journal lines, on the other hand, we want to update the linked customer payment record when the amount in the payment journal lines is modified.

The event handler is implemented in a function, UpdateCustomerPaymentOnModifyJnlLine, of codeunit **50515 Lease Contract Events**. Modify the function properties, given as follows:

- **Event**: Subscriber
- **EventPublisherObject**: Table Gen. Journal Line
- **EventFunction**: OnAfterModifyEvent

In the function body, we check that the journal line is the payment and that the line amount has changed, the same as we did for sales invoices. If confirmed, search the related customer payment record and update it. The event subscriber function updating the payment on modification is as follows:

```
[EventSubscriber(Table,81,OnAfterModifyEvent)]
LOCAL PROCEDURE UpdateCustomerPaymentOnModifyJnlLine(
  VAR Rec : Record 81;VAR xRec : Record 81;RunTrigger : Boolean);
VAR
  CustomerPayment : Record 50502;
  CustPaymentGenJnlLine : Record 50504;
BEGIN
  IF (Rec."Document Type" <> Rec."Document Type"::Payment) OR (Rec.Amount =
xRec.Amount) THEN
    EXIT;
```

```
WITH CustPaymentGenJnlLine DO BEGIN
  SETRANGE("Gen. Jnl. Template Name",Rec."Journal Template Name");
  SETRANGE("Gen. Jnl. Batch Name",Rec."Journal Batch Name");
  SETRANGE("Gen. Jnl. Line No.",Rec."Line No.");
  IF FINDFIRST THEN BEGIN
    CustomerPayment.GET("Customer Payment Entry No.");
    CustomerPayment.VALIDATE(Amount,Rec.Amount);
    CustomerPayment.MODIFY(TRUE);
  END;
END;
END;
```

In the next event subscription example, we want to block the deletion of customers that have active contracts or unprocessed payments. We also don't want to allow the deleting of active contracts, as well as contracts that are not completely paid.

It's easy for contracts, since we can control our own code and modify it as we please. For example, modify the `OnDelete` trigger in table **50500 Lease Contract Header**:

```
IF CustomerPaymentsMgt.UnprocessedContractPaymentsExist("No.") THEN
  ERROR(UnprocessedPmtErr,"No.");

CALCFIELDS("Total Amount");
IF CustomerPaymentsMgt.CalculateAmountPaidAtDate(Rec,0D) < "Total Amount"
THEN
  IF NOT CONFIRM(DeleteContractQst) THEN
    ERROR('');

LeaseContractLine.SETRANGE("Contract No.","No.");
LeaseContractLine.DELETEALL(TRUE);
```

Two text constants are used in this code sample. Declare them in C/AL Globals as per the following table:

Name	ConstValue
DeleteContractQst	Contract is not completely paid. Do you want to delete it?
UnprocessedPmtErr	Unprocessed payments exist for contract %1. Contract cannot be deleted.

The `UnprocessedContractPaymentsExist` function referenced in the previous code sample has not been declared yet. Create this function in codeunit **50504 Customer Payments Mgt.**, as shown in the next code snippet:

```
PROCEDURE UnprocessedContractPaymentsExist(ContractNo : Code[20]) :
Boolean;
VAR
  CustomerPayment : Record 50502;
BEGIN
```

```
  CustomerPayment.SETRANGE("Contract No.",ContractNo);
  CustomerPayment.SETRANGE("Journal Line Posted",FALSE);
  EXIT(NOT CustomerPayment.ISEMPTY);
END;
```

This is what needs to be done to control the deletion of contracts. But we don't own the **Customer** table , and would prefer to avoid changing its source code. This means that we have to subscribe to database events triggered by this table. Before we continue with event subscriptions, we need two helper functions that will check for existing unpaid contracts and unposted payments.

Both functions are declared in codeunit **50504 Customer Payments Mgt.**. First, create the UnpaidCustomerContractsExist function. Make it global by changing the **Local** property from **Yes** to **No**:

```
PROCEDURE UnpaidCustomerContractsExist(CustomerNo : Code[20]) : Boolean;
VAR
  LeaseContractHeader : Record 50500;
BEGIN
  LeaseContractHeader.SETRANGE("Customer No.",CustomerNo);
  IF LeaseContractHeader.FINDSET THEN
    REPEAT
      LeaseContractHeader.CALCFIELDS("Total Amount");
      IF CalculateAmountPaidAtDate(LeaseContractHeader,0D) <
    LeaseContractHeader."Total Amount" THEN
        EXIT(TRUE);
    UNTIL LeaseContractHeader.NEXT = 0;

  EXIT(FALSE);
END;
```

Then, create the second helper function, UnprocessedCustomerPaymentsExist, in the same codeunit, **Customer Payments Mgt**. This function should also be globally available. Here is the function code:

```
PROCEDURE UnprocessedCustomerPaymentsExist(CustomerNo : Code[20]) :
Boolean;
VAR
  LeaseContractHeader : Record 50500;
BEGIN
  LeaseContractHeader.SETRANGE("Customer No.",CustomerNo);
  IF LeaseContractHeader.FINDSET THEN
    REPEAT
      IF UnprocessedContractPaymentsExist(LeaseContractHeader."No.") THEN
        EXIT(TRUE);
    UNTIL LeaseContractHeader.NEXT = 0;
```

```
EXIT(FALSE);
END;
```

The event subscriber itself is a function, `BlockDeleteOnDeleteCustomer`, in codeunit **50515 Lease Contract Events**. Create this function and set the subscription properties as follows:

- **Event**: `Subscriber`
- **EventPublisherObject**: `Table Customer`
- **EventFunction**: `OnBeforeDeleteEvent`

The `BlockDeleteOnDeleteCustomer` will invoke helper functions declared in the the codeunit 50504; therefore, a codeunit variable will be required. Since the codeunit consolidates functions related to lease contracts, and will be used only as a static variable, it is reasonable to declare it in the global scope. In the **Lease Contract Events** codeunit, open the C/AL Globals declarations and create the global variable that is described in the next table:

Name	DataType	Subtype
CustomerPaymentsMgt	Codeunit	Customer Payments Mgt.

Two text constants will be required to store error messages. Declare these in C/AL Globals as well. The next table shows the required constants:

Name	ConstValue
UnpaidContractErr	Unpaid contracts exist for customer %1.\Customer cannot be deleted.
UnprocessedPaymentErr	Unprocessed payment exist for customer %1.\Customer cannot be deleted.

Now, we can proceed with the `Subscriber` function and write its code:

```
[EventSubscriber(Table,18,OnBeforeDeleteEvent)]
LOCAL PROCEDURE BlockDeleteOnDeleteCustomer(VAR Rec : Record 18;RunTrigger
: Boolean);
BEGIN
  IF CustomerPaymentsMgt.UnpaidCustomerContractsExist(Rec."No.") THEN
    ERROR(UnpaidContractErr,Rec."No.");

  IF CustomerPaymentsMgt.UnprocessedCustomerPaymentsExist(Rec."No.") THEN
    ERROR(UnprocessedPaymentErr,Rec."No.");
END;
```

UI events

Like the database trigger events described in the previous section, page trigger events are not raised by C/AL code, but initiated by the NAV platform. UI events are triggered in response to user actions in different UI controls. These events are closely related to traditional page triggers generated by pages and page controls.

To see how to use this type of event, we will extend the functionality of the action button **Post** on the **39 General Journal** page. As the name implies, the **Post** button runs the **Gen. Jnl.-Post** batch job. Suppose we want to augment this function by opening the list of G/L entries posted by the job. Since what we want to do is perform a UI extension, it is logical to use UI events for this purpose.

We will place the new event subscriber in the same codeunit, **Lease Contract Events**, we used for event subscribers before. Create a function in the codeunit and assign a name to it: ShowEntriesOnAfterJournalPost. As for the other event subscribers, a UI subscriber should point to the publisher object and the corresponding event function. Modify the following properties to establish this link:

- **Event**: Subscriber
- **EventPublisherObject**: Page General Journal
- **EventFunction**: Select OnAfterActionEvent and confirm the overwrite of the method signature

After this action, you will see one more property in the list: **EventPublisherElement**. This is the name of the action button that will provide the event entry point. Select **Post** from the list of page action elements as the value of the EventPublisherElement property .

Now, the ShowEntriesOnAfterJournalPost function will be executed after users push the **Post** button in the general journal line, and posting completes. The code of the function is shown as follows:

```
[EventSubscriber(Page,39,OnAfterActionEvent,Post)]
LOCAL PROCEDURE ShowEntriesOnAfterJournalPost(VAR Rec : Record 81);
VAR
  GLRegister : Record 45;
  GLEntry : Record 17;
  GeneralLedgerEntries : Page 20;
BEGIN
  GLRegister.SETRANGE("User ID",USERID);
  IF GLRegister.FINDLAST THEN BEGIN
    GLEntry.SETRANGE("Entry No.",GLRegister."From Entry No.",GLRegister."To
Entry No.");
    GeneralLedgerEntries.SETTABLEVIEW(GLEntry);
```

```
        GeneralLedgerEntries.RUN;
    END;
  END;
```

This code will be executed after the action's `OnPush` trigger, which means that the moment out extension code is called, journal posting is already completed and the G/L register saved. We can find the last register record marked with the current user ID and open a page showing its G/L entries.

`OnQueryClosePage` is another example of a page trigger often modified in custom solutions. It is typically used to request confirmation to close the page. With UI events, we can raise the same request without modifications to the page object.

Let's extend the **Item** page to verify that the user has entered a unit price when editing an item record. First of all, we will need a text constant with a request that will be shown to the user to request confirmation. Declare this constant in codeunit **50515 Lease Contract Events**. The following table shows the constant to be created:

Name	ConstValue
`ConfirmPageCloseQst`	Item unit price is not specified. Close the page anyway?

In the same codeunit, add a function, `ConfirmOnItemCardQueryClosePage`, and set the subscription properties, given as follows:

- **Event**: `Subscriber`
- **EventPublisherObject**: `Page Item Card`
- **EventFunction**: `OnQueryClosePageEvent`

Then, return to the C/AL code editor and add code to the function as follows:

```
[EventSubscriber(Page,30,OnQueryClosePageEvent)]
LOCAL PROCEDURE ConfirmOnItemCardQueryClosePage(VAR Rec : Record 27;VAR
AllowClose : Boolean);
BEGIN
  IF Rec."Unit Price" = 0 THEN
    AllowClose := CONFIRM(ConfirmPageCloseQst);
END;
```

A new `EventSubscriber` is executed before closing the page, and the item record being edited is passed to the function in the `Rec` parameter. With the item, we can check that it has the `Unit Price` filled in, and if not, we remind the user to set it right. The value assigned to the second parameter, `AllowClose`, is returned to the platform and indicates whether the page should be closed or not.

The last example of UI events we will discuss now aids in extending another widely used page `OnNewRecord` trigger,. This time, the page that is going to be extended is **Customer**. We will assign default values to the **Payment Terms Code** and **Payment Method Code** item fields when a new record is created on the page. But to be able to assign default values, we need these values to be configured in a setup table. Let's create a setup table for the lease contracts add-on to see how this is usually handled in NAV.

Create a new table with the fields listed:

Field No.	Field Name	Data Type	Length
1	Primary key	Code	10
2	Default Payment Terms Code	Code	10
3	Default Payment Method Code	Code	10

This is the module setup table. Save it with the ID and name **50505 Lease Contract Setup**. This type of table always has one field named **Primary Key**, which is the table's primary key. The value of this field is always blank since a setup table can contain only one record.

Create a new page for the setup interface. Create the page using the wizard and choose card for the page type. Two of the table fields will be shown on the page. Include **Default Payment Terms Code** and **Default Payment Method Code** in the page layout. **Primary Key** remains hidden from the user.

Setup pages always contain a single record that cannot be deleted, and new records cannot be inserted. Because of this, such pages have the values of two properties set to **No**: **InsertAllowed** and **DeleteAllowed**. The one and only record in the underlying table must be inserted programmatically. Usually, setup tables are created by data migration tools, such as RapidStart, when a new company is created. Add-on developers often supplement their solutions with initialization procedures or wizards.

But if the setup is not provided by data migration tools, the record is inserted on opening the setup page. This is a pattern of setup initialization. To conform with the pattern, insert this code in the **OnOpenPage** of page **50508 Lease Contract Setup**:

```
RESET;
IF NOT GET THEN BEGIN
  INIT;
  INSERT;
END;
```

When the setup is ready, we can move on to the page event subscriber, adding new functionality to the `OnNewRecordEvent`. In the codeunit `Lease Contract Events`, create an `InitializeCustomerOnNewRecord` function and configure its properties to subscribe to the event publisher `OnNewRecordEvent` of the `Item` page. The properties to be configured are the following:

- **Event**: `Subscriber`
- **EventPublisherObject**: `Page Customer Card`
- **EventFunction**: `OnNewRecordEvent`

In the following function code, assign values received from the setup table to the corresponding item fields:

```
[EventSubscriber(Page,21,OnNewRecordEvent)]
LOCAL PROCEDURE InitializeCustomerOnNewRecord(
  VAR Rec : Record 18;BelowxRec : Boolean;VAR xRec : Record 18);
VAR
  LeaseContractSetup@1003 : Record 50505;
BEGIN
  IF NOT LeaseContractSetup.GET THEN
    EXIT;

  IF Rec."Payment Terms Code" = '' THEN
    Rec."Payment Terms Code" := LeaseContractSetup."Default Payment Terms
Code";

  IF Rec."Payment Method Code" = '' THEN
    Rec."Payment Method Code" := LeaseContractSetup."Default Payment Method
Code";
END;
```

`OnNewRecordEvent` is raised after the page's own `OnNew` record trigger is executed, so in this event handler we can amend the initial record values before it is inserted into the table.

Publishing custom events

The NAV event model is not limited to events provided by the base application code or raised in response to system triggers. Developers can extend the model by raising their own events. To raise an event, you need to create a publisher function and call in your code where the event should be triggered. In this section, we will publish several events associated with specific actions on lease contracts.

Event publisher function

The event publisher function itself does not contain any code. We declare a publisher function to define its signature and identify the place in the code where the event is triggered. We will raise custom events on invoice and journal line creation in codeunit 50504 **Customer Payments Mgt.**. The first one is `OnBeforeCreateInvoice`, which is to be triggered when the creation of an invoice from the contract is invoked, but before the document is created.

The first step in raising an event is to create a function carrying the event signature. Declare a function, `OnBeforeCreateInvoice`, in codeunit **50504 Customer Payments Mgt.** with one parameter, as shown in the following code sample:

```
[Integration]
LOCAL PROCEDURE OnBeforeCreateInvoice(LeaseContractHeader : Record 50500);
BEGIN
END;
```

The `LeaseContractHeader` function parameter is the record variable that will be sent from the event publisher to the subscriber; it will carry the source contract for the invoice. This record will be passed by the code raising the event. We will learn how to do this in the next half of this section.

When the function is declared, set up the event properties, given as follows:

- **Event**: `Publisher`
- **EventType**: `Integration`

By creating this function, we have defined the event signature. Let's create other event headers before moving on to the event raising part. The second event must be raised when the invoice is created. Still in the same codeunit, declare a function, `OnAfterCreateInvoice`, which is the next invoice-related event. See the next code block for the event signature:

```
[Integration]
LOCAL PROCEDURE OnAfterCreateInvoice(LeaseContractHeader : Record
50500;SalesHeader : Record 36);
BEGIN
END;
```

In this and all following event publisher functions that will be declared in this section, set up the same properties as follows:

- **Event**: Publisher
- **EventType**: Integration

This event provides two parameters to the subscriber, the first being the source contract record, as in the OnAfterCreateInvoice event, and the second parameter being the invoice, which will have been created by the moment the OnAfterCreateInvoice event is called.

Similar events will be raised for invoice lines. The third event we create in the **Customer Payments Mgt.** codeunit is OnBeforeCreateInvoiceLine. It will send the related lease contract line to the subscriber, and this line should be declared as a parameter of the event publisher function:

```
[Integration]
LOCAL PROCEDURE OnBeforeCreateInvoiceLine(LeaseContractLine : Record
50501);
BEGIN
END;
```

Another event publisher function, OnAfterCreateInvoiceLine, should be declared in the same codeunit. This one will be called after creating the invoice line, and the prepared line is passed in event arguments to the subscriber:

```
[Integration]
LOCAL PROCEDURE OnAfterCreateInvoiceLine(LeaseContractLine : Record
50501;SalesLine : Record 37);
BEGIN
END;
```

Raising events

Now, we have all required event publisher functions in place and can raise events in the application code. All we need to do to raise an event is invoke the corresponding publisher function that was declared earlier.

To raise `OnBeforeCreateInvoice` and `OnAfterCreateInvoice` events, modify the `CreateSalesInvoice` function in the codeunit **50504 Customer Payments Mgt.**. Add two function calls, `OnBeforeCreateInvoice` at the very beginning of the function, and `OnAfterCreateInvoice` before the `EXIT` statement:

```
PROCEDURE CreateSalesInvoice(VAR LeaseContractHeader : Record 50500) :
Code[20];
VAR
  SalesHeader : Record 36;
BEGIN
  OnBeforeCreateInvoice(LeaseContractHeader);
  CreateSalesInvoiceHeader(SalesHeader,LeaseContractHeader);
  CreateSalesInvoiceLines(SalesHeader,LeaseContractHeader."No.");
  OnAfterCreateInvoice(LeaseContractHeader,SalesHeader);

  EXIT(SalesHeader."No.");
END;
```

From this code, you can see why `OnBeforeCreateInvoice` sends only the contract header to its subscribers, while `OnAfterCreateInvoice` adds a sales header to the list of arguments. The first event is triggered when the sales invoice is not available.

The same modification must be made in the `CreateSalesInvoiceLines` function . The first event is called at the start of each iteration of the loop, when the new invoice line is not yet initialized, and the second raised after creating the line. New event calls are highlighted in bold in the code block:

```
LeaseContractLine.SETRANGE("Contract No.",ContractNo);
IF LeaseContractLine.FINDSET THEN
  REPEAT
    OnBeforeCreateInvoiceLine(LeaseContractLine);
    LineNo += 10000;
    SalesLine.VALIDATE(Type,SalesLine.Type::Item);
    SalesLine.VALIDATE("No.",LeaseContractLine."Item No.");
    SalesLine.VALIDATE(Quantity,1);
    SalesLine.VALIDATE("Line Amount",LeaseContractLine.Amount);
    SalesLine.INSERT(TRUE);
    OnAfterCreateInvoiceLine(LeaseContractLine,SalesLine);
  UNTIL LeaseContractLine.NEXT = 0;
END;
```

Now, you can save the codeunit and try subscribing to your new custom events. The process is no different from subscribing to system integration events. The next section will present manual subscription to events, as opposed to automatic subscription, which we have used so far, and will also illustrate subscription to custom events.

Manual event subscription

In all event subscribers we created in this chapter, subscription was activated as soon as the `Subscriber` function was saved and compiled. But this is not necessary; subscription can be started manually by C/AL code. Now, we will see how to activate subscription on demand.

This example will subscribe to a custom event raised on the creation of a general journal line from a customer payment record. We will use it to show a progress bar window with the number of processed lines. Event subscription will help separate the user interface (progress window) from the line-processing code, and enable the window when needed simply by activating the subscription.

Journal lines are created in codeunit **50504 Customer Payments Mgt.** by the `CreatePaymentJournalLines` function, which is given as follows:

```
PROCEDURE CreatePaymentJournalLines(VAR CustomerPaymentFilter : Record
50502);
VAR
  CustomerPayment : Record 50502;
BEGIN
  CustomerPayment.COPYFILTERS(CustomerPaymentFilter);
  CustomerPayment.SETRANGE("Journal Line Created",FALSE);
  IF CustomerPayment.FINDSET THEN
  REPEAT
    CreatePaymentJournalLine(CustomerPayment);
  UNTIL CustomerPayment.NEXT = 0;

  CustomerPayment.MODIFYALL("Journal Line Created",TRUE);
END;
```

`CreatePaymentJournalLines` loops through customer payments and invokes `CreatePaymentJournalLine` on each iteration of the loop. In this function, we will embed the call to the event that will help us update the progress window.

The `CreatePaymentJournalLine` function called in the loop is shown as follows:

```
LOCAL PROCEDURE CreatePaymentJournalLine(CustomerPayment : Record 50502);
VAR
  GenJournalLine : Record 81;
BEGIN
  // Code of this function is described in Chapter 5,Exchanging data with
XML Ports
  OnAfterCreatePaymentJnlLine(GenJournalLine);
END;
```

To be able to call the event, we must declare the stub function carrying its signature in the same codeunit, 50504. The event signature is shown here:

```
[Integration]
LOCAL PROCEDURE OnAfterCreatePaymentJnlLine(VAR GenJournalLine : Record
81);
BEGIN
END;
```

One more function is required in codeunit 50504: `GetLinesCountToProcess`. This function must be declared as global, since it is going to be used in other objects. Its purpose is to count the number of records to be processed in the **Customer Payment** table:

```
PROCEDURE GetLinesCountToProcess(VAR CustomerPaymentFilter : Record 50502)
: Integer;
VAR
  CustomerPayment : Record 50502;
BEGIN
  CustomerPayment.COPYFILTERS(CustomerPaymentFilter);
  CustomerPayment.SETRANGE("Journal Line Created",FALSE);
  EXIT(CustomerPayment.COUNT);
END;
```

Now, let's create the event subscriber that is going to manage the window status. For this, we will need a new codeunit. The subscriber cannot be placed in the **Lease Contract Events** codeunit used previously, because we want to manage the subscription manually, and the subscription method is defined by the properties of the codeunit itself and cannot be changed for a single method.

Create a codeunit and assign it the ID and name **50516 Lease Contract UI Handler**. Open the codeunit's properties. The one we are interested in now is **EventSubscriberInstance**. Its default value, assigned automatically, is **Static-Automatic**, which means that all event subscribers declared in this codeunit will be activated automatically. Change the value to **Manual** to disable automatic activation, and do it in your C/AL code.

When the codeunit is created and the subscription method is configured, declare the following global variables in it:

Name	DataType	Subtype
CustomerPaymentsMgt	Codeunit	Customer Payments Mgt.
Window	Dialog	
ProcessedLinesCount	Integer	
WindowUpdateThreshold	Integer	

One global text constant is required for the code example:

Name	ConstValue
ProcessedLinesTok	No. of lines processed: #####1# out of #####2#.

With all variables and constants in place, let's get on with creating functions for controlling the window appearance. The first of theses functions is `OpenLineCountWindow`, which initializes the window and sets the update threshold for it. `UpdateTheshold` defines how often the window will be updated:

```
PROCEDURE OpenLineCountWindow(TotalLinesCount : Integer;UpdateThreshold :
Integer);
BEGIN
  Window.OPEN(ProcessedLinesTok);
  Window.UPDATE(2,TotalLinesCount);
  WindowUpdateThreshold := UpdateThreshold;
END;
```

The counterpart of the `OpenLineCountWindow` function is `CloseLineCountWindow`, which simply calls `Window.CLOSE` on the window instance. This function is to be created in codeunit **50516 Lease Contract UI Handler**; its code is as follows:

```
PROCEDURE CloseLineCountWindow();
BEGIN
  Window.CLOSE;
END;
```

And now, we come to the main part of the process: the event subscriber method. Subscriber function `UpdateCountOnJournalLineCreated`, similar to all the function described in this section, should be declared in codeunit **50516 Lease Contract UI Handler.**

In its properties, set the following values:

- **Event**: `Subscriber`
- **EventPublisherObject**: `codeunit Customer Payments Mgt.`
- **EventFunction**: `OnAfterCreatePaymentJnlLine`

The following code block shows the event subscriber code:

```
[EventSubscriber(Codeunit,50504,OnAfterCreatePaymentJnlLine)]
LOCAL PROCEDURE UpdateCountOnJournalLineCreated(VAR GenJournalLine : Record
81);
BEGIN
  ProcessedLinesCount += 1;
  IF ProcessedLinesCount MOD WindowUpdateThreshold = 0 THEN
    Window.UPDATE(1,ProcessedLinesCount);
END;
```

For the event publisher, we selected our custom event triggered in the **Customer Payments Mgt.** codeunit after creating payment journal lines, and now `UpdateCountOnJournalLineCreated` will be called every time a line is inserted in the journal. But the codeunit is configured for manual event subscription, and the subscriber is not going to be invoked while it is inactive.

The subscription will be activated on page **50507 Customer Payments**. The `Subscriber` method will use two global variables that should be declared in the page object. The variables to be declared are in the next table:

Name	DataType	Subtype
CustomerPaymentsMgt	Codeunit	Customer Payments Mgt.
LeaseContractUIHandler	Codeunit	Lease Contract UI Handler

Now, modify a `CreatePaymentJnlLines` function, which is invoked on the action **Create Journal Lines** as per the following code block:

```
LOCAL PROCEDURE CreatePaymentJnlLines();
BEGIN
LeaseContractUIHandler.OpenLineCountWindow(CustomerPaymentsMgt.GetLinesCoun
tToProcess(Rec),1);
  BINDSUBSCRIPTION(LeaseContractUIHandler);
  CustomerPaymentsMgt.CreatePaymentJournalLines(Rec);
  UNBINDSUBSCRIPTION(LeaseContractUIHandler);
  LeaseContractUIHandler.CloseLineCountWindow;
END;
```

In this function, all preparations we did in the **Lease Contract UI Handler** codeunit are combined to open the window, activate the subscription before creating the set of lines, deactivate it after, and finally close the window.

`OpenLineCountWindow` receives the total number of payment lines to be processed and the `UpdateThreshold` parameter. In the previous sample code, the threshold was set to 1, which means that the window will be updated after creating each payment line. This is probably too often and could slow down the process if the number of lines is high. In this case, the threshold can be changed to some larger value, for example 10, to update the status on each tenth line.

The `BINDSUBSCRIPTION` function activates event subscribers declared in the codeunit passed to it as an argument. It stays active until the codeunit goes out of scope, or `UNBINDSUBSCRIPTION` is called. The code example explicitly deactivates the subscription by calling `UNBINDSUBSCRIPTION`. After this line, **Lease Contract UI Handler** is deactivated and the `UpdateCountOnJournalLineCreated` subscriber is not called on new lines.

To complete the process, the function closes the window, which is not needed anymore.

Summary

This chapter detailed the structure of application events raised by C/AL code, as well as events triggered by the platform in response to system events to UI actions. It explained how business application developers can use events to integrate their extension code into a base application, without modifications to base objects. We also learned to raise custom events and subscribe in automatic or manual mode.

In the next chapter, we will enrich the application with various reports, design a report layout, use RDLC scripts for client-side logic, and create interactive reports.

Presenting Data in Reports

7

Reports are always among the key requirements set for an ERP system. The ability to present data in an informative and well-structured way, and the possibility to quickly develop a report, are inevitably demanded from the system. Microsoft Dynamics NAV comes with a built-in report designer, which enables the developer to structure the dataset. The dataset is further carried over to the external layout designer, where dataset fields and variables are bound to the presentation layer.

Thus, the development of a NAV report is split into two phases: the data preparation step in the NAV report designer, and the report layout design, which is effected in Microsoft Visual Studio or Report Builder for SQL Server.

Now, we will take a tour of the different types of reports that can be created in NAV and cover the topics listed here:

- Preparing a report dataset
- Modeling a report layout
- Report triggers
- Designing a report request page
- RDLC expressions
- Interactive reports
- Data items based on temporary tables

Preparing a report dataset

Before we can start designing the report layout, which is going to be presented to the user, we must prepare the data structure for it. In order to do this, we create a report object in the NAV object designer. As for any other object, switch the object designer to the report view and push *Ctrl + N* or run the **File | New** action from the main menu.

The dataset designer itself is quite simple and similar in many aspects to the XMLport designer. The designer is basically a table in which you select tables, fields, and variables that the report will be based on. Parameters you fill in for each data element are as follows:

- **Data Type**: Can take one of two values, **DataItem** or **Column**, and defines the type of the data source, which is defined in the next column.
- **Data Source**: Data element that will provide data for the element. Press *Shift + F2* in this field to open the **C/AL Symbols** menu and choose the data provider.
- **Name:** Data source name that will be used in the layout designer. This parameter is explained in detail in the *Modeling a report layout* section.

If you select **Column** as the data type, it does not mean that the data source must be a table column. It can also be a variable or even a function call.

Now, we can start preparing the dataset for our first NAV report, which will show a list of customers with their contracts, as well as amounts paid and owed by the customers. Using the **C/AL Symbols** menu, create the data items structure, as shown in the next table. Make sure that all indentations are observed: all fields of type **Column** must be aligned under the respective data item. Use the arrow buttons located under the dataset table to move data items:

Data Type	Data Source	Name	Include Caption
DataItem	**Customer**	**Customer<Customer>**	No
Column	Customer."No."	CustomerNo	Yes
Column	Customer.Name	CustomerName	Yes
DataItem	**Lease Contract Header**	**<Lease Contract Header>**	No
Column	"Lease Contract Header"."No."	ContractNo	Yes
Column	"Lease Contract Header"."Starting Date"	StartingDate	Yes
Column	"Lease Contract Header"."Ending Date"	EndingDate	Yes
Column	"Lease Contract Header"."Total Amount"	TotalAmount	Yes
Column	"Lease Contract Header"."Amount Paid"	AmountPaid	Yes
DataItem	**Lease Contract Line**	**<Lease Contract Line>**	No
Column	"Lease Contract Line"."Item No."	ItemNo	Yes
Column	"Lease Contract Line".Description	LineDescription	Yes
Column	"Lease Contract Line".Amount	LineAmount	Yes

Don't forget to fill in the **Include Caption** field ; this will be required when we start designing the layout, and serves to bind field captions to report column headers. A configured list of tables and table fields is shown in the next screenshot. At the bottom of the page, you can see the buttons that are used to rearrange data elements:

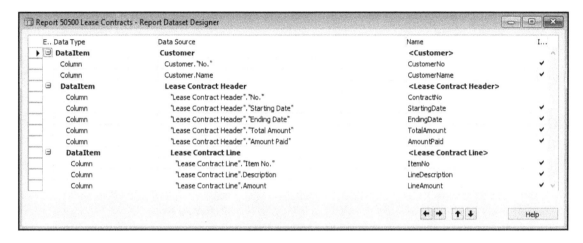

Report Dataset Designer

When all data source items are in place, we can establish links between data items. And once again, this is an analogue of what did earlier for XMLports; the execution logic and link setup interfaces are still the same.

To configure data item links, follow these steps:

1. Select the **Lease Contract Header** data item and open its properties.
2. Locate the **DataItemLink** property and push the assist button in the **Value** column.
3. In the **DataItem Link** window, select the **Customer No.** field in the **Field** column, and **No.** for the **Reference Field**.
4. Push OK. This slightly contradicts common NAV user experience, but if you simply close the window, changes will not be saved.
5. Now, close the data item properties and select the next data item that must be linked: **Lease Contract Line**.
6. Repeat step 1 to step 3 to link the **Contract No.** of the contract line with the **No.** field of the contract header.

The next screenshot demonstrates the setup window and the configured link between the data items **Lease Contract Line** and **Lease Contract Header**:

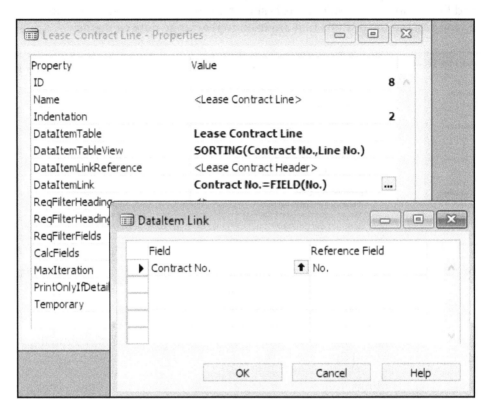

DataItem Link configuration

All this setup we've just described means that from now on, records of the **Contract Header** table will be filtered by the customer number, and a filter on the **Contract No.** field will be applied to the **Contract Line** table.

When the report is run, the first record of the top-level data item is retrieved from the database. After that, all records of the underlying data item are processed one by one and the execution proceeds with the next record of the top-level data item. Thus, the processing order for the report 50500 is going to look like this:

- Customer 1
    - Contract 1
        - Lines of Contract 1
    - Contract 2
        - Lines of Contract 2
- Customer 2
    - Contract 3
        - Lines of Contract 3

Two of the fields included in the report dataset are FlowFields, which means that their values are not stored in the database, but must be calculated on the fly. These fields are **Total Amount** and **Amount Paid**. To obtain the values of these fields, we could employ a trigger and call the system **CalcFields** function. But there is an alternative way—set up the property **CalcFields** to make the report calculate fields automatically. Simply open the properties of the **Lease Contract Header** data item and select the fields from the list or enter the field names manually in the **CalcFields** property.

The final thing that we must do in the dataset designer is include a text string that will be displayed as the report header. Activate the **View** | **Labels** menu action and enter the name and the caption for the report label:

- **Name:** ReportName
- **Caption:** Customer Contracts

Close the page and save the report. We are moving on to the next step: visual data presentation.

Modeling a report layout

The dataset is prepared, and now we are ready to launch the next phase of report development: turning the raw data into a presentable graphical view. In this part of our development experience, we step away from the NAV object designer, as the layout design is carried out in an external editor.

While the underlying dataset is the responsibility of NAV, the presentation layer is a **Report Definition Language Client Side** (RDLC) report project, which is designed and executed by external components.

Layout design

At this point, we still need the NAV object designer to start the RDLC report designer. To begin creating the report layout, open the report object in the NAV report designer and run the **View** | **Layout** menu action.

 To edit the RDLC report layout, Report Designer for Visual Studio or Report Builder for SQL Server is required.

The default report layout editor configured for NAV is Visual Studio. If you prefer to use SQL Server Report Builder, the default configuration must be changed. To switch your editor to Report Builder, open the code editor options (**Tools** | **Options** in the top application menu) and change the **Use Report Builder** to **Yes** key.

A new RDLC report project is created upon starting the report designer. This project already contains all the necessary files; we don't need to bother about the project structure and can start drawing the report. All the tools that will be required for the layout design are collected in the **Toolbox** pane. If the toolbox is not open when you start the report designer, you can access it via the top menu action **View** | **Toolbox**, or by pressing *Ctrl* + *Alt* + *X*.

The basic element of all the report presentation structure is the **Table** control; it will display records from all data items that we included in the report during the data structure design. With the Toolbox pane on the screen, drag and drop the **Table** item from the toolbox to the report canvas.

Now, the shiny new table must be linked to a data source, which will provide a data feed for the report. The following steps explain how to establish a link:

1. Right-click on the table header.
2. Choose the **Tablix Properties** action from the drop-down menu.
3. In the **General** tab of the **Tablix Properties** window, set the value of the **Dataset name** field. The NAV report project always contains one dataset, named **DataSet_Result**.

The following screenshot illustrates the blank table component and its context menu:

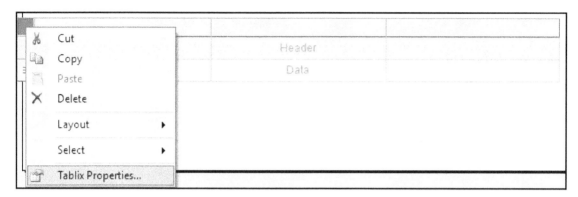

Table properties

A generic RDLC report is not limited to a single table; it can contain several tables, each receiving data from its own data source. When designing a NAV report, we always have a single data source that is provided by NAV itself.

After placing the table component on the report canvas and defining the dataset link, we can start binding table controls to dataset fields. A new table, just created from the toolbox, is divided into three columns. For this report, we need eight, so before connecting columns with data fields, let's insert additional columns into the table control. Right-click on any column and in the context menu, select the **Insert Column** submenu. This submenu has two action items: a new column can be inserted on the right or on the left of the selected column. Since we do not have any data bindings so far, it does not matter where we insert a new column. Select any action: **Insert Column** | **Left** or **Insert Column** | **Right**. Repeat the action until you reach the required column count, eight columns.

Now, let's add data sources to table columns. Hover the mouse cursor over the table cell you have just inserted and click the icon in the top-right corner of the cell, as shown in the following screenshot:

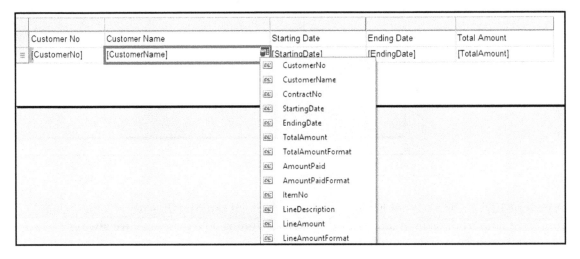

Selecting the data source for a table cell

The drop-down menu in the screenshot shows a list of all fields in the data source bound to the table. Starting from the leftmost cell of the table, choose the data source fields for all columns:

- **CustomerNo**
- **CustomerName**
- **ContractNo**
- **StartingDate**
- **EndingDate**
- **ItemNo**
- **LineDescription**
- **LineAmount**

These are all the data fields we need to show in the report. But to make it more informative, we can combine lines into groups and show group totaling. At the bottom of the report layout designer, you can see two panels: **Row Groups** and **Column Groups**. In the **Row Groups** panel, right-click on **Details**, choose the **Add Group** menu, and then choose the **Parent Group** option:

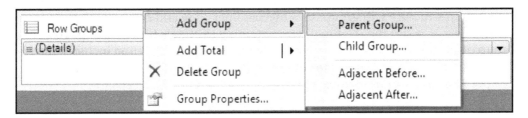

Tablix group

In the **Tablix group** window that will be opened, select **Group by** and choose the
CustomerNo dataset field from the drop-down menu. When you choose and confirm the
grouping field, it is automatically added to the table; you don't have to insert
the **CustomerNo** into the layout.

But besides the customer number, we want to show the customer name, and table rows
should be grouped by customer name as well. Select the **CustomerNo** field in the table,
then right-click on the field header. In the drop-down menu, select the **Insert Column |
Inside Group - Right** action.

The **Row Group** created previously will arrange table rows with the same customer
number. In this report, we want to add another level; contract lines must be grouped by the
contract number, within the customer group. Repeat the action described previously to add
another parent group for **Details**, and select the **ContractNo** field as the **Group by**
parameter. Now, the Row Groups section has the following structure:

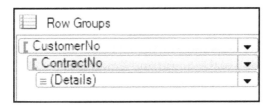

Report Row Groups

This row group structure will group lines by customer code and contract number. In any of the groups, we can insert the totaling lines containing subtotals for the group. To add totals in a group, right-click any field of the **Details** section (now, this section includes the **Item No**, **Line Description**, and **Line Amount** fields). In the context menu, select the action **Insert Row** | **Inside Group - Below**. This menu is shown in the screenshot:

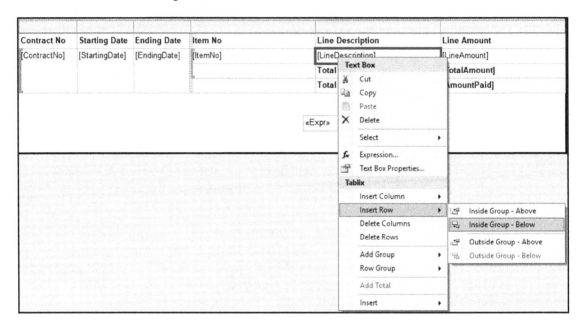

Creating report totaling rows

Create two lines inside the group and link them to data sources; these fields will receive data from the totaling fields **TotalAmount** and **TotalPaid**.

Now, we are done with the table structure, but several data fields still remain unassigned. First of all, this is the report title. There is a text label still waiting to be linked to a header field. The title will be placed in the report header. Right-click on the report body and choose **Insert** | **Page Header**.

In the header, we will insert the report title and the date of its generation. We will run ahead of the normal course of events here and use RDLC expressions to display the date. Expressions are explained in detail later in this chapter.

First, the title. Drag an drop the **Text Box** control from the toolbox to the header, then right-click on the control and select **Expression...**. The **Expression** window will open, allowing you to edit the **Report Definition Language** (**RDL**) expression for the selected control. The window is divided into four panes. The top pane contains the source expression itself, and here you can enter and edit it manually. Three panes at the bottom of the window are **Category**, **Item**, and **Values**. Here, you can browse through different data sources and build simple expressions with several mouse clicks. Select the **Parameters** category in the left pane. In the **Item** pane, the only option available is **All**, and it is selected by default. This option will include all report parameters passed into the dataset. Finally, in the **Values** pane, choose **ReportName** and double-click on it. The source expression will be displayed in the **Expression** pane: `=Parameters!ReportName.Value`.

Following the same pattern, drag and drop another text box to the report header and set the source expression for it. This textbox should show the current date, and the date functions are grouped under the **Common Functions** | **Date & Time** category. Select this category, and choose the **Now** function in the **Item** pane. When you double-click on the function name, the value you you will see in the expression value is `=Now`.

After completing all the setup in the header, right-click in the report body and select **Insert** | **Page Footer**. In the footer, we want to show the page number on each report page. Drag and drop a textbox to the page footer, right-click on it, and open the textbox source expression. This time, we are going to edit the expression manually and combine two functions in one expression to show the current page number and the total page count. The RDLC function `PageNumber` returning the current page number can be found in the **Built-in Fields** category. The total page count resides under **Built-in Fields** | **TotalPages**. To show both fields in the same textbox, concatenate two values in the **Expression** as follows: `="Page " & Globals!PageNumber & " of " & Globals!TotalPages`.

When rendered, this expression will show the current page number and the total page count of a text: `Page 1 of 4`.

Formatting data output

The report layout is ready, all amounts are calculated, and the UI controls have data sources. Still, if you run the report right now, the output will not be very clean: numeric fields display unexpected numbers of decimal signs; dates come in conjunction with time values that do not make any sense. To make a long story short, the data fields lack proper formatting.

Save your changes in the RDLC report designer now, as we are going to take one step back and return to the native NAV report designer. Save the changes and close Visual Studio. The NAV development environment keeps the report object locked while it is open in the Visual Studio. After you return to the NAV report designer, it will inform you that the object was changed by another application and request confirmation to import changes. While you are working on the report layout in Visual Studio, modifications are saved in a temporary file that must be imported into the NAV object.

 If you do not confirm the request, all changes to the report layout made in Visual Studio will be lost.

In the NAV object designer, the formatting of numeric fields is defined by field properties: **AutoFormatType**, **AutoFormatExpr**, and **DecimalPlaces**. In the NAV report data structure, we have three numeric fields: **Lease Contract Header.Total Amount**, **Lease Contract Header.Amount Paid**, and **Lease Contract Line.Amount**. By default, the **AutoFormatType** property is set to zero for all fields, and **DecimalPlaces** is undefined. **AutoFormatType 0** is fine for us; it means that the formatting of the number is defined by system settings, and only the number of decimal places can be identified by the field properties. For all three decimal fields, change the **DecimalPlaces** property to **2:2**. The two numbers divided by the semicolon are the minimum and maximum number of decimal places that should be displayed in the field. With these settings, there will always be two decimal digits in all numeric fields.

The following screenshot illustrates the resulting report output:

Customer No	Customer Name	Contract No	Starting Date	Ending Date	Item No	Line Description	Line Amount
01905893	Candoxy Canada Inc.	LC0002	01.01.2018	24.03.2019	766BC-A	CONTOSO Conference System	5 413.18
						Total	5 413,18
						Total paid	1 587,00
21245278	Maronegoce	LC0001	01.01.2018	24.03.2019	1936-S	BERLIN Guest Chair, yellow	125,10
						Total	248,40
					1972-S	MUNICH Swivel Chair, yellow	123,30
						Total	248,40
						Total paid	444,00
		LC0003	01.01.2018	24.03.2019	766BC-C	CONTOSO Storage System	944,91
						Total	1 068,21
					1972-S	MUNICH Swivel Chair, yellow	123,30
						Total	1 068,21
						Total paid	12 636,00
27489991	Durbandit Fruit Exporters	LC0004	13.03.2018	12.05.2019	1720	Hand front wheel Brake	125,00
						Total	125,00
						Total paid	0,00

Report output

Report triggers

Like other C/SIDE objects, reports allow full functional capabilities for extension and customization. C/AL code can be executed in report triggers to control the data flow, and in this section you will learn how to use the most common triggers to tailor the report output to your needs.

When the report object is executed, its triggers run in the following order:

- OnInitReport: Executed before the report object is initialized.
- OnPreReport: Executed after initializing the object, but before reading any data from the database.
- OnPreDataItem: Executed before initializing the dataset for a data item. This trigger is a good place for filtering the dataset if you need to apply a filter dynamically, instead of setting it in the **DataItemTableView** property.
- OnAfterGetRecord: Executed after the record is retrieved from the database.
- OnPostDataItem: Executed after processing all records in the dataset.
- OnPostReport: Executed after processing all data items in the report.

Now, we are going to use the OnPreReport trigger to collect the filters applied to the report and show filters in the layout. Modify the report, **50500 Lease Contracts**, we just created and declare a global variable in it: ReportFilters: Text.

To access the report trigger code, press *F9* or select the menu action **View** | **C/AL Code**. In the OnPreReport trigger, add one line, as shown in the following code:

```
OnPreReport()
  ReportFilters := Customer.GETFILTERS;
```

Now, this variable containing the filter string must be included in the report dataset to be passed to the layout designer. All we need to do to make it a part of the dataset is insert a new line in the report dataset designer and specify the variable as the data source. Add a line under the **Customer** data item as follows:

Data Type	Data Source	Name
Column	ReportFilters	ReportFilters

When it's done, open the report layout designer and add a textbox in the report header. Right-click on the textbox and open the expression editor. The ReportFilters variable can be found under **Datasets** | **DataSet_Result** | **First(ReportFilters)**. Double-click on the value; the code that will be pasted in the **Expression** pane is =First(Fields!ReportFilters.Value, "DataSet_Result").

This is what is takes to initialize a variable in a report trigger and display its value in the layout. Now, let's see how we can use triggers to skip records that we don't want to show in the report. In the **Lease Contracts** report, the top-level data item is **Customer**, and the report will list all customers in the output, including those that do not have any contracts. There is no filter that can be applied to show only customers with contracts, but the `OnAfterGetRecord` trigger can help fix this.

Open the code editor and locate the **Customer**, `OnAfterGetRecord` trigger. Declare a local variable in the trigger, as per the following table:

Name	DataType	Subtype
LeaseContractHeader	Record	Lease Contract Header

Write the code from the next code block in the trigger:

```
Customer - OnAfterGetRecord()
  LeaseContractHeader.SETRANGE("Customer No.",Customer."No.");
  IF LeaseContractHeader.ISEMPTY THEN
    CurrReport.SKIP;
```

This function is called after retrieving each record from the **Customer** table. For each record, it analyzes whether the customer has contracts in the **Lease Contract Header** table. If there are no contracts, the customer will be skipped and not shown in the report. To skip a record, the `CurrReport.SKIP` function is used. Here, `CurrReport` is a system variable in the report object; it always refers to the report itself.

Other applications of the `OnAfterGetRecord` trigger will be illustrated in another report. Now, we are done with the **Lease Contracts** report. Create a new report and save it as **50501 Customer Payment Dates** report. In this new report, we will show the expected payment dates for each customer contract.

Build the report structure as the next table shows:

Data Type	Data Source	Name
DataItem	**Customer**	**<Customer>**
Column	Customer."No."	CustomerNo
Column	Customer.Name	CustomerName
DataItem	**Lease Contract Header**	**<Lease Contract Header>**
Column	Lease Contract Header"."No."	ContractNo
Column	NextPaymentDate	NextPaymentDate

Define the **DataItemLink** property for the **Lease Contract Header** data item. It should link customers with their contracts: `Customer No.=FIELD(No.)`.

`NextPaymentDate` here is a variable that does not exist yet. So, open C/AL Globals and declare two global variables:

Name	Data Type	Subtype
CustomerPaymentsMgt	Codeunit	Customer Payments Mgt.
NextPaymentDate	Date	

Add the code that will calculate the value of the payment date in the **Lease Contract Header** trigger, `OnAfterGetRecord`, as shown in the following code block. This line calculates the value of the variable for each contract when the **Lease Contract Header** record is retrieved from the database:

```
Lease Contract Header - OnAfterGetRecord()
   NextPaymentDate := CustomerPaymentsMgt.CalcNextPaymentDate("Lease
Contract Header"."No.",WORKDATE);
```

For the **Customer**, `OnAfterGetRecord` we will use the same code as in the previous report to skip customers that don't have active contracts:

```
Customer - OnAfterGetRecord()
   LeaseContractHeader.SETRANGE("Customer No.",Customer."No.");
   IF LeaseContractHeader.ISEMPTY THEN
     CurrReport.SKIP;
```

As in the previous report, open the report labels (**View** | **Labels**) and create the following text label:

Name	Caption
ReportTitle	Next payment date

Now the preparation is done, you can go to the report layout designer and create the layout. Fields that should be shown in the report are shown in this screenshot:

Customer payment dates report layout

Right-click on the report title textbox and choose the **Text Box Properties...** option. In the properties window that opens, select the **Font** tab and increase the font size to 12 pt, and tick the **Bold** checkmark. It's also a good idea to separate column headers from data by showing them in bold as well.

NextPaymentDate, which is a **DateTime** field, should also be assigned a special format, since we only want to see the date and not the time. **Text Box Properties** | **Number** | **Date**. OK.

Designing a report request page

Every time you run a report, you see a page that prompts you to set filters on data items. This is a report request page, and its functions are wider then a just setting filters on underlying data items. Any parameters you want to pass to the report can be entered through its request page. On the other hand, we can reduce the number of default parameters requested by the page. A separate filtering section in the report request page is shown for each data item. It does not make sense for many reports and clutters the interface with useless elements. For example, in the reports created so far, we don't need to filter contract lines and would like to remove that section from the request page.

To remove filter sections you don't need on the page, just set the value of the **DataItemTableView** property for the report data item. It is sufficient to select an active key.

Now, we will continue designing report **50501 Customer Payment Dates** and replace standard filtering options with a custom parameter. Action items are listed as follows to explain how to select an active key for a data item:

1. Select the **Lease Contract Header** data item.
2. Open the data item properties and select the **No.** key in the **DataItemTableView** property.

When you save and run the report, only filters on the **Customer** table will be available on the request page. We already did this for XMLport request pages, and like in XMLports, in report request pages developers can ask users to enter additional parameters.

An additional parameter that we will add in the **Customer Payment Dates** report is **Show Overdue Only**. With this option checked, the report will show only overdue payments. Otherwise, all contracts will be displayed.

Declare a global variable in the report: ShowOverdueOnly: Boolean.

The request page designer is already familiar to you; this is the same editing interface used to develop request pages for XMLports, and basically the usual page designer. Open it by calling **View** | **Request Page** menu items. The default action container is already present in the page structure; you just need to give it a name. Let's name it **Parameters**. Enter the name in the **Name** column.

Under the container definition, insert another line (its default type is **Field**, and this is what we need). Fill in the other parameters as follows:

Type	SubType	SourceExpr	Name	Caption
Container	ContentArea		Parameters	<Parameters>
Field		ShowOverdueOnly		Show Overdue Only

A Boolean variable will be required for the next code sample. Declare it in the report's **C/AL Globals**: IsOverdue—Boolean. Actually, it could be a local variable in the trigger, but it will be also used later in RDLC expressions, so let's make it global. Now, amend the code in the OnAfterGetRecord trigger, as shown in the next code snippet:

```
Lease Contract Header - OnAfterGetRecord()
  NextPaymentDate := CustomerPaymentsMgt.CalcNextPaymentDate("Lease
Contract Header"."No.",WORKDATE);
  IsOverdue := CustomerPaymentsMgt.IsOverduePayment("Lease Contract
Header"."No.");
  IF ShowOverdueOnly AND NOT IsOverdue THEN
    CurrReport.SKIP;
```

This code works fine when we need to skip contracts, but there is an issue here: code in the **Lease Contract Header**—OnAfterGetRecord trigger is executed only after the customer record is processed. This means that we cannot skip customers that have no contracts which must be reported, and a customer record will still be shown in the report event if this customer does not have overdue payments. There are different possibilities to work around this issue, and one of them is post-processing the dataset with RDLC expressions, which is explained in the next section.

RDLC expressions

We already touched upon the RDLC expression editor in previous sections of this chapter. Now, let's take a look at other applications of client-side report expressions.

One of the most common functions implemented by RDLC expressions is showing or hiding report rows and columns based on a condition. Let's see how to hide a certain report line and give the user an option to hide totaling values in report **50500 Lease Contracts**. Modify the report and create two global variables: ShowTotalPaid—Boolean and ShowTotalContract—Boolean.

These variables must be shown in the request page controls. Open the request page designer (**View | Request Page**) and add the controls in the page structure:

Type	SourceExpr	Name	Caption
Container		Parameters	\<Parameters>
Field	ShowTotalContract	ShowTotalContractControl	Show Total Contract
Field	ShowTotalPaid	ShowTotalPaidControl	Show Total Paid

Default values of both variables should be initialized to TRUE; by default all totals are present in the report, but it is possible to disable them. To assign initial values, we will employ another report trigger, OnInitReport:

```
OnInitReport()
   ShowTotalContract := TRUE;
   ShowTotalPaid := TRUE;
```

Close the code editor and add the new variables to the report dataset. To include values in the dataset, insert new lines in the dataset designer under the Customer data item:

Data Type	Data Source	Name
Column	ShowTotalPaid	ShowTotalPaid
Column	ShowTotalContract	ShowTotalContract

Run the layout designer (**Vew | Layout**). In the designer, select the report row that has the **TotalAmount** field as the source. Right-click on the line and choose the **Row Visibility** menu action, as shown in the following screenshot:

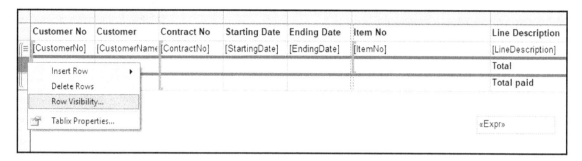

Customer No	Customer	Contract No	Starting Date	Ending Date	Item No		Line Description
[CustomerNo]	[CustomerName]	[ContractNo]	[StartingDate]	[EndingDate]	[ItemNo]		[LineDescription]
							Total
							Total paid
							«Expr»

Insert Row ▶
Delete Rows
Row Visibility...
Tablix Properties...

Row visibility menu

Follow these steps to set the row visibility condition:

1. In the display option, select the **Show or hide based on an expression** option, then push the expression button next to the textbox.
2. In the expression editor, choose the **Datasets** category.
3. **DataSet_Result** is the only available option for Item.
   Select **First(ShowTotalContract)** in the **Values** pane and double-click on the value.
4. Amend the expression copied to the editor pane, as shown in this code block:

```
=not First(Fields!ShowTotalContract.Value, "DataSet_Result")
```

The report row will be hidden when the expression is evaluated to true, and displayed if the evaluation result is false.

Push OK to accept the new expression, then return to the layout editor, select the line for `AmountPaid`, and repeat the same steps, selecting the `ShowTotalPaid` field in the **Values** pane. The resulting expression for the visibility of `AmountPaid` is as follows:

```
=not First(Fields!ShowTotalPaid.Value, "DataSet_Result")
```

RDLC expressions come in handy when report output must be formatted dynamically, depending on the data. For example, let's modify the **Customer Payment Dates** report and highlight overdue contract payments, similar to was was done to highlight overdue payments on the page:

1. Here, we need the `IsOverdue` variable to be present in the report dataset. To include it in the dataset, insert a **Column** element under the **Lease Contract Header** data item and choose `IsOverdue` in the **Data Source**.

2. The value of the global `ShowOverdueOnly` variable must also be sent to RDLC processing. Repeat the first step for this variable to include it in the dataset.

3. Right-click `NextPaymentDate`. Go to the Font tab. Push the button in front of the **Color** field.

4. In the Expression pane, enter the following code:

```
=iif(Fields!IsOverdue.Value,"Red","Black")
```

This expression will assign a color to the field depending on the value of the `IsOverdue` field. If the first parameter of the `iif` expression is evaluated to true, the text will be displayed in red; otherwise, it will be black.

> Do not move the application logic to RDLC unless there is no way to implement it on the C/AL side. RDLC expressions are very difficult to debug.

Interactive reports

RDLC reports enable developers to add interactive capabilities to reports. In this section, we will see how to add sorting buttons to the generated report and allow end users to sort the output by any of the report columns. To do this, we will modify the **Customer Payment Dates** report. The default report layout sorts the data by customer number. But probably users want to see the list sorted by customer name or the payment date instead; with RDL, we can give them this option. First, let's add sorting to the **Customer No.** column, which is our default sorting key:

1. Right-click on the textbox containing the header of the first column: **Customer No.**. It is important that the sorting property is enabled on the header textbox, not the data field.

2. Select **Text Box Properties** from the drop-down menu and choose the **Interactive Sorting** tab in the properties window.

3. Enable the checkmark in the **Enable interactive sorting on this text box** field.

4. In the **Sort by** field, select the name of the field that is going to be the sorting key: **[CustomerNo]**.

The next screenshot illustrates the Text Box Properties window, where you can set up sorting parameters:

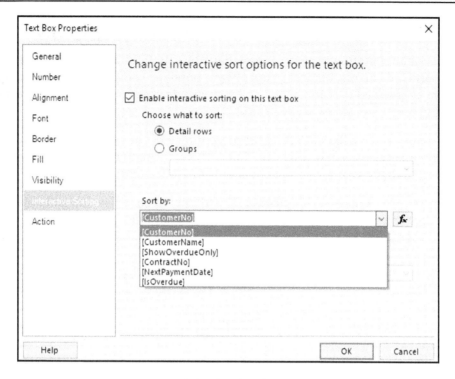

Setting up interactive sorting

Now, repeat the same steps for all the fields you want to use as sorting keys.

You can do data sorting based on an RDLC expression. Just click the
expression button next to the Sort By field and enter the expression in the
editor.

When the report is run, you will see a sorting button in the column headers (see the
following screenshot). When you click on a button, the report output will be ordered by the
respective column:

Customer No	⇕	Customer Name	⇕	Contract No	⇕	Next Payment Date	⌃
21245278		Maronegoce		LC0001		29.01.2018	
01905893		Candoxy Canada Inc.		LC0002		01.02.2018	
21245278		Maronegoce		LC0003		01.02.2018	
27489991		Durbandit Fruit Exporters		LC0004		13.03.2018	

Report with sorting buttons

Data items based on temporary tables

In all reports created in this chapter, we took data directly from a table and mapped table fields to report UI elements. But this is not always possible; complicated analysis reports often require aggregated data that cannot be simply extracted from a table, but requires preprocessing.

In the next example, we will create a report presenting a list of customers with quarterly payment amounts calculated for each customer. This information is not stored anywhere in the database; amounts have to be calculated and stored in a temporary table.

Create a report, **50502 Quarterly Payments**. The following table lists the global variables required in the report. Declare these variables in C/AL Globals:

Name	DataType	Subtype
TempCustomer	Record	Customer
TempCustomerPayment	Record	Customer Payment
StartingDate	Date	
EndingDate	Date	
EntryNo	Integer	
Amount	Decimal	

`TempCustomer` and `TempCustomerPayment` are temporary records; set **Temporary** to **Yes** in both variables' properties. The amount is an array. For this variable, access the properties and change the value of the **Dimensions** property to **4**. Four elements of the array will be filled with payment amounts—one per quarter.

If you export the object after declaring all variables, the list of global variables should look like this:

```
VAR
   TempCustomer : TEMPORARY Record 18;
   TempCustomerPayment : TEMPORARY Record 50502;
   StartingDate : Date;
   EndingDate : Date;
   EntryNo : Integer;
   Amount : ARRAY [4] OF Decimal;
```

Create the report dataset structure as per this table:

Data Type	Data Source	Name
DataItem	Integer	\<Integer\>
Column	TempCustomer."No."	CustomerNo

Column	TempCustomer.Name	CustomerName
Column	Amount[1]	Q1Amount
Column	Amount[2]	Q2Amount
Column	Amount[3]	Q3Amount
Column	Amount[4]	Q4Amount

The root data item in this dataset is a virtual table, **Integer**; it is not to be found anywhere in the database. It's simply a list of integer numbers presented in the form of a Record object to be used as an iterator. You can declare a variable of this type, apply filters, and find records as for a normal record. Here, we will use the Integer virtual table to iterate over the records in temporary tables. We need this separate iterator, because temporary tables cannot be used as data items in reports.

Write the following code in the report `OnPreDataItem` trigger :

```
OnPreDataItem=BEGIN
  CollectCustomerPaymentsBuffer;
  Integer.SETRANGE(Number,1,TempCustomer.COUNT);
  IF TempCustomer.FINDSET THEN
    FindCustomerPayments(TempCustomer."No.");
END;
```

The first line of the code snippet calls the `CollectCustomerPaymentsBuffer` function (its source code follows) where the two temporary tables are filled with precalculated customer payments. In the next line, the Integer table is filtered to limit the number of iterations on the root data item. The number of iterations must exactly match the number of records in the `TempCustomer` buffer table. With this filter applied, code in the `Integer – OnAfterGetRecord` trigger will be executed as many times as defined by the `COUNT` function.

Now, let's move on to the `OnAfterGetRecord` trigger and add the following code:

```
OnAfterGetRecord=BEGIN
  IF Integer.Number > 1 THEN
    TempCustomer.NEXT;
  FindCustomerPayments(TempCustomer."No.");
END;
```

When we use a normal table as a report data item, we don't have to take care when reading the next record in a table; the NAV server does it for us. In the case of a temporary table, synchronization of the active record is the developer's responsibility. This trigger reads the next record from the `TempCustomer` table, then calls the `FindCustomerPayments` function to sync records in `TempCustomerPayment` with the active customer record.

Now, let's declare the main function that calculates aggregated amounts per quarter for each customer. The code of the function is in the next code block:

```
LOCAL PROCEDURE CollectCustomerPaymentsBuffer();
VAR
   Customer : Record 18;
   CustomerPayment : Record 50502;
   Date : Record 2000000007;
   PeriodNo : Integer;
BEGIN
   IF Customer.FINDSET THEN
     REPEAT
       CustomerPayment.SETRANGE("Customer No.",Customer."No.");
       CustomerPayment.SETRANGE("Payment Date",StartingDate,EndingDate);
       IF NOT CustomerPayment.ISEMPTY THEN BEGIN
         TempCustomer := Customer;
         TempCustomer.INSERT;

         PeriodNo := 0;
         Date.SETRANGE("Period Type",Date."Period Type"::Quarter);
         Date.SETRANGE("Period Start",StartingDate,EndingDate);
         Date.FINDSET;
         REPEAT
           PeriodNo += 1;
           EntryNo += 1;
           CustomerPayment.SETRANGE("Payment Date",Date."Period
           Start",Date."Period End");
           CustomerPayment.CALCSUMS(Amount);
           TempCustomerPayment."Entry No." := EntryNo;
           TempCustomerPayment."Customer No." := Customer."No.";
           TempCustomerPayment."Payment Date" := Date."Period Start";
           TempCustomerPayment.Amount := CustomerPayment.Amount;
           TempCustomerPayment.INSERT;
         UNTIL Date.NEXT = 0;
       END;
     UNTIL Customer.NEXT = 0;
   END;
```

Here, we use another virtual table: Date. Like the **Integer** table, the date is maintained by the system and isn't stored in the database. It contains date periods that can be grouped by applying filters on the table. We use it to find starting and ending dates of four quarters. First, we set a filter on the period type we want to find: Date.SETRANGE("Period Type",Date."Period Type"::Quarter). The next filter is set on the period starting date; we only want to find periods in the year requested by the user: Date.SETRANGE ("Period Start",StartingDate,EndingDate). And finally, Date.FINDSET selects all quarters in the filtered date period.

The next function, `FindCustomerPaymentDates`, retrieves aggregated amounts from the buffer table; this function is called from the `OnAfterGetRecord` trigger to synchronize customer records and related payment amounts:

```
LOCAL PROCEDURE FindCustomerPayments(CustomerNo : Code[20]);
VAR
  Date : Record 2000000007;
  I : Integer;
BEGIN
  Date.SETRANGE("Period Type",Date."Period Type"::Quarter);
  Date.SETRANGE("Period Start",StartingDate,EndingDate);
  Date.FINDSET;
  FOR I := 1 TO ARRAYLEN(Amount) DO BEGIN
    TempCustomerPayment.SETRANGE("Customer No.",CustomerNo);
    TempCustomerPayment.SETRANGE("Payment Date",Date."Period Start");
    IF TempCustomerPayment.FINDFIRST THEN
      Amount[I] := TempCustomerPayment.Amount;

    Date.NEXT;
  END;
END;
```

One more thing we need to do on the C/AL side is add the starting and ending dates of the reporting period to the report request page. The global variables `StartingDate` and `EndingDate` are declared for this purpose; now, let's initialize these variables and prompt the user to enter the required dates.

Create a function in the report object as per the following code block:

```
LOCAL PROCEDURE UpdateReportDates(PivotDate : Date);
BEGIN
  StartingDate := CALCDATE('<-CY>',PivotDate);
  EndingDate := CALCDATE('<CY>',PivotDate);
END;
```

In this function, we initialize starting and ending dates to the first and the last day of the year, respectively.

On opening the request page, we will initialize the dates to span the current year, enabling the user to change the date filter. Open the request page designer (**View** | **Request Page**), and from here, switch to the C/AL code editor. In the `OnOpenPage` trigger, add the following code:

```
OnOpenPage=BEGIN
  UpdateReportDates(WORKDATE);
END;
```

If you open the C/AL code editor from the dataset designer, the request page triggers are not available. The code editor must be accessed from the request page designer for page triggers to be visible.

In the `StartingDateControl` trigger —`OnValidate`, add the following code:

```
OnValidate=BEGIN
  UpdateReportDates(StartingDate);
END;
```

Also, a similar line should be present in the `EndingDateControl` trigger—`OnValidate`, but with a slight change: the parameter passed to the function will be `EndingDate`, so the function call is `UpdateReportDates(EndingDate)`.

With all the preparation completed, switch to the report layout designer and create the layout as shown in the screenshot:

Customer No	Customer Name	Q1 Amount	Q2 Amount	Q3 Amount	Q4 Amount
[CustomerNo]	[CustomerName]	[Q1Amount]	[Q2Amount]	[Q3Amount]	[Q4Amount]

Quarterly payments report layout

Now, you can run the report and review the payments received from customers, aggregated by quarter.

Summary

This chapter demonstrated several examples of NAV reporting capabilities. We created a simple report, presenting records in a list, as well as more complicated reports with data aggregates, groups, and client-side expressions.

The last chapter is going to give you a short overview of C/SIDE debugging tools.

Debugging Your Code 8

The ability to analyze code and find errors when something goes wrong in the application is one of the essential requirements of any development environment. The basic set of tools necessary for debugging is mostly the same in all popular integrated development environments and includes the ability to break code execution at a given point, run statements one by one, and review the environment state at each step.

The final chapter of this book provides an overview of the debugging capabilities offered by C/SIDE and introduces you to the following topics:

- Activating the debugger
- Breakpoints
- Conditional breakpoints
- Variables, Watches, and Callstack
- Capturing code coverage

Activating the debugger

If you have ever developed code in a popular development environment, such as Microsoft Visual Studio, IntelliJ IDEA, Eclipse, or other similar IDEs, your first experience with the NAV debugger may seem unusual. Usually, a debugger starts within the same interface as the code editor and attaches to the application thread started from the same environment. In Dynamics NAV, the debugger is activated in two steps. First, start the session list in the code editor (choose the menu action **Tools | Debugger | Debug Session**). This action opens a window with a list of NAV client sessions currently running on the same computer. To start the debugger, choose the session you want to debug from the list and press **Debug**.

The next screenshot illustrates the debugger window:

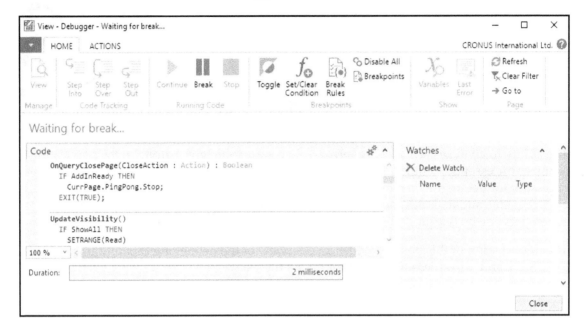

Debugger window

If there are no running sessions, this button will be inactive. You can press **Debug Next**; the debugger window will start without a connection to a NAV session, but will wait for a session to start. The debugger will connect to the first activated session and open a separate window where the code being debugged is shown. This is not typical for integrated development environments, where a debugger usually shares an interface with the editor. In NAV, the editor and debugger are separated.

The buttons on the page include the following:

- **Break**: Pause current execution and start debugging the session.
- **Continue**: Continue executing the code until the end or the next break event.
- **Stop**: Terminate code execution and exit debug mode. If there is an active transaction, it will be rolled back.
- **Step Into**: Execute the statement under the cursor. If the statement is a C/AL function and its source code is available, the debugger will enter this function and continue debugging it line by line.

- **Step Over**: Like the previous function, Step Over executes the statement under the cursor. This action will not step into the function, but will execute the line in one step.
- **Step Out**: Exit the current function being debugged and continue debugging from the next statement following the function.

Run the client, then activate the debugger and push **Break**. If you are running the application on a NAV demo database with a default setup, the debugger will stop on the page **681 Report Inbox Part**. This page hosts a component called PingPong, which probes the server every ten seconds to check if there are new reports to be displayed in the inbox.

Breakpoints

Breakpoints are an important part of any debugger. They allow the developer to pause code execution on a predefined line of code to continue execution step by step, while reviewing all the changes of the variables after each step. Since the NAV debugger is separated from the code editor, the breakpoints interface is also quite unusual compared to most popular development environments.

Now, we will complete a short walkthrough and try debugging one of the previously developed reports.

Activating breakpoints

A breakpoint in C/AL code can be set in the code editor, as well as in the debugger window. Open a C/AL object in the designer and locate the code you want to scrutinize under the debugger. For example, let's debug one of the reports we developed: report **50502 Quarterly Payments**. To set a breakpoint in the `CollectCustomerPaymentsBuffer` function, do as follows:

1. Open report 50502 in the report designer.
2. Access the C/AL code editor.
3. Position the cursor on the line where you want to pause the code execution.
4. Press *F9* to set the breakpoint. The activated breakpoint can be disabled and deleted with the same button, *F9*.

The code editor with an active breakpoint is shown in the screenshot:

```
20 ⊟Integer - OnPostDataItem()
21  |
22 ⊟LOCAL CollectCustomerPaymentsBuffer()
23  | IF Customer.FINDSET THEN
24  |   REPEAT
25  |     CustomerPayment.SETRANGE("Customer No.",Customer."No.");
26  |     CustomerPayment.SETRANGE("Payment Date",StartingDate,EndingDate);
27  |     IF NOT CustomerPayment.ISEMPTY THEN BEGIN
28  |       TempCustomer := Customer;
29  |       TempCustomer.INSERT;
```

Code editor with a breakpoint

Continue with the previous example to stop the debugger at the breakpoint.

5. Now, save the report and close the editor.
6. Activate the debugger and connect it to the active session, as described in the first section of this chapter.
7. Execute the object from the object designer window; the debugger will break execution at the marked line, and here you can review the values of the variables within the current scope. We will come back to the variables soon in this chapter.

You can review all active and disabled breakpoints if you push the **Breakpoints** button on the debugger page. This button opens a page with a list of all breakpoints (both enabled and disabled), their location in code, and the break conditions.

Break rules

Other events besides breakpoints can break code execution and activate the debugger. There are three types of these events, and break conditions for each type of event can be set up under **Break Rules**.

Mentioned break conditions include the following options:

- **Break on error**: Break execution when an error occurs. This can be caused by an exception (for example, division by zero or incorrect type cast), or by the explicit call of an error function (ERROR, FIELDERROR, TESTFIELD).
- **Break on record changes**: Break execution when a record is inserter, deleted, or modified.
- **Skip Codeunit 1**: Do not stop on events raised by Codeunit 1.

Codeunit 1 has been removed from the application in Dynamics NAV 2019, and the last option does not exist either.

Conditional breakpoints

A conditional breakpoint is a breakpoint with a conditional expression assigned to it. The expression value is evaluated every time the debugger reaches the breakpoint. The debugger breaks code execution on a conditional breakpoint only when its expression is evaluated to true.

To set a conditional breakpoint and break code execution at that point, perform the following steps:

1. Open the **50502 Quarterly Payment** report in the report designer, then activate the C/AL code editor
2. Set a breakpoint inside the REPEAT .. UNTIL loop
3. Save the report, activate the debugger, and run the report
4. When the debugger breaks on the breakpoint you set, push the **Set/Clear Condition** button
5. Enter the break condition, for example, Customer."No." = '20000'

With the condition described here, the execution will break on the breakpoint when the customer record with No. = 20000 is read from the table. When the break condition is set, the pictogram of the breakpoint changes to a red dot with a white cross inside to indicate that there is a condition associated with the breakpoint.

One thing you should remember when applying conditions on breakpoints is that you can include FlowFields in the condition expression, but values of these fields must be calculated in C/AL code. For example, if you want to break execution when a customer with a balance exceeding 1,000 is found, you could write an expression for the break condition: Customer.Balance > 1000. But in report 50502, this condition is never going to be satisfied, since the customer balance is a FlowField that is never calculated in the report. It will only work if you add a line, Customer.CALCFIELDS(Balance), before the breakpoint.

Operators that can be used in breakpoint conditions include these:

- =
- <>
- <
- <=
- >
- >=

To remove a condition you don't need anymore, do as follows:

1. Position the cursor on the code line with the breakpoint.
2. Press **Set/Clear Condition** to open the condition expression dialog.
3. Delete the condition expression and confirm the dialog.

Variables – Watches – Callstack

The ability to break code execution at a certain point does not help in finding bugs by itself. Breakpoints are one tool in the developer's toolbox when it comes to code analysis. When the code flow is on pause, it is time to take a closer look at the state of the application. And two important tools that allow you to look deeper into the application are Variables and Watches.

Let's see what information we can get from these windows. Once again, we are going to use the **50502 Quarterly Payments** report as an example. Run the report and pause its execution on the `CollectCustomerPaymentsBuffer` function, as explained in the *Activating breakpoints* section. Now, you can review all variables in this function's visibility—global variables of the report object and local declarations in the function. Push the **Variables** action button to open the **Debugger Variable List** window. Here, you can see the list of local variables. Globals are also shown in the same window, but under the category Globals. Expand the Globals section to see all global variables.

For each variable, you can view its type and value. For a Record type variable, some additional information is available. Here is what you can see in the Variables for a Record variable:

- Fields
- Filter Group
- Filters
- Keys
- Global variables and global text constants of the record object

While the **Debugger Variables** interface provides detailed information on visible variables, it is inconvenient to open a window after every debugger step when you want to monitor the variable's value. To keep the variable in sight, select it in the Debugger Variable List and push **Add Watch**. The selected variable will be moved to the **Watches** list, which is always visible (unless you remove it from the page) and displays only selected variables. The Watches window lacks flexibility, which the Variables list can give you—you cannot unfold a record variable down to its fields, but have to add record fields to Watches on by one. On the other hand, it allows the developer to concentrate on the information necessary at that moment.

The following screenshot shows the **Watches** window with several variables added to it:

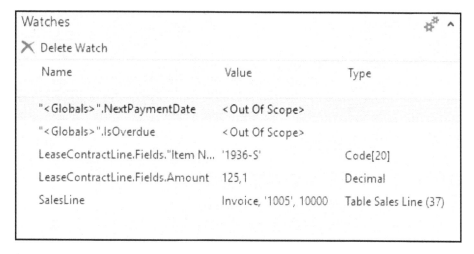

Watches window

Note that global variables always have a prefix, **<Globals>**, preceding the variable name. Record fields and filters have an explicit indication on the value category. For example, the field **Item No.** of the record variable **LeaseContractLine** is shown as **LeaseContractLines.Fields."Item No."**, although the intermediate keyword Fields does not exist in C/AL code.

Variables can also be added to the Watches list directly from the debugger. Hover the mouse cursor over a variable name: the debugger will show you the variable type, value, and scope. The small plus sign in the same hint (see the following screenshot) will send the variable to the Watches:

```
Code
    CollectCustomerPaymentsBuffer()
    | IF Customer.FINDSET THEN
        REPEAT
            CustomerPayment.SETRANGE("Customer No.",Customer."No.");
            CustomerPayment.SETRANGE("Payment Date",StartingDate,EndingDate);
            IF NOT CustomerPayment.ISEMPTY THEN BEGIN
                TempCustomer := Customer;
                TempCustomer.INSERT;

                PeriodNo := 0;
                Date.SETRANGE("Period Type",Date."Period Type"::Quarter);
                Date.SETRANGE("Period Start",StartingDate,EndingDate);
                Date.FINDSET;
                REPEAT                          Globals
                    PeriodNo += 1;                  EndingDate (Date) = 31.12.18
                    EntryNo += 1;
                    CustomerPayment.SETRANGE("Payment Date",Date."Period Start",Date."Period End");
```

Viewing variable values in the debugger window

Capturing code coverage

Code coverage analysis is a very useful tool when it comes to identifying which code has been executed in a particular application run. A typical situation in which a developer turns to the code coverage tool is when a record is modified or inserted, and the source of the change is unknown. You push just one button, but there is a huge amount of code hidden underneath it, and it can be tough to identify the particular line of code that modified the record. To narrow down the search, we can capture code coverage to see which lines of code were actually executed when a particular action was triggered.

The code coverage tool is activated from the client application, not from the code editor. To run it, start the NAV client and navigate to **Departments** | **Administration** | **Code Coverage**. To collect code coverage, follow these steps:

1. Push **Start** to run the code coverage. Now, the tool is active and traces code execution in the same client session.
2. Run the function you want to monitor. Let's continue debugging report 50502. Just run the report and click **Preview**.
3. When done, return to the code coverage window and push **Stop**.

When code coverage monitoring is stopped, all coverage information appears in the window, as the next screenshot illustrates:

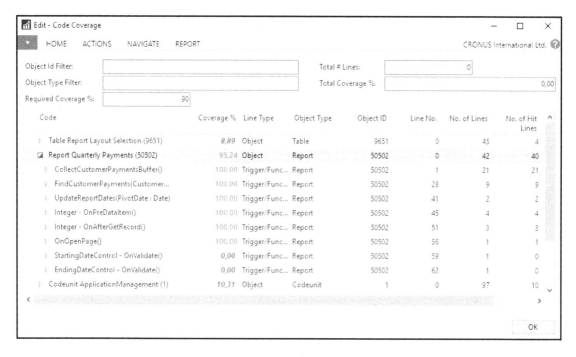

Code coverage information

This window displays all objects that were executed while the code coverage monitor was active. Even if only a single line of code in an object was executed, it will appear in the list. The **Coverage %** metric is calculated for each object as the number of code lines that were executed in the object, divided by the total number of lines. For example, in the screenshot we can see that the **Quarterly Payments** report contains 42 code lines, and 40 of these were executed during the run. The coverage percentage is calculated as *40 / 42 * 100% = 95.24%*.

The code presented in the **Code Coverage** window is structured in a tree view: you can expand any object to the list its functions, and any function to view its separate code statements.

Summary

This short detour into the debugging capabilities of NAV competes the *Quick Start Guide to Dynamics NAV development*. In the last chapter of this book, you found out how to use the C/SIDE debugger and learned some code debugging tricks. The key tools that were presented were breakpoints, Watches, and code coverage.

Other Books You May Enjoy

If you enjoyed this book, you may be interested in these other books by Packt:

Microsoft Dynamics 365 Enterprise Edition - Financial Management (Third Edition)
Mohamed Aamer

ISBN: 9781788839297

- Examine the business logic behind the financial functionalities of Microsoft Dynamics 365 FFO
- Set up and configure the core modules of financial management
- Grasp the key control points of financial management
- Explore intercompany and consolidation in Microsoft Dynamics 365 FFO
- Understand multi-currency sales, tax mechanisms, and budgeting capabilities in Microsoft Dynamics 365 FFO
- Get to grips with month/year-end period close functionality
- Understand the account payable and receivable module
- Use Microsoft Dynamics 365 to create financial reports

Dynamics 365 Business Central Development Quick Start Guide
Stefano Demiliani

ISBN: 9781789347463

- Develop solutions for Dynamics 365 Business Central
- Create a sandbox for extensions development (local or on cloud)
- Use Docker with Dynamics 365 Business Central
- Create extensions for Dynamics 365 Business Central
- Handle dependencies, translations and reporting
- Deploy extensions on-premise and to the cloud
- Create serverless processes with Dynamics 365 Business Central
- Understand source code management for AL

Leave a review - let other readers know what you think

Please share your thoughts on this book with others by leaving a review on the site that you bought it from. If you purchased the book from Amazon, please leave us an honest review on this book's Amazon page. This is vital so that other potential readers can see and use your unbiased opinion to make purchasing decisions, we can understand what our customers think about our products, and our authors can see your feedback on the title that they have worked with Packt to create. It will only take a few minutes of your time, but is valuable to other potential customers, our authors, and Packt. Thank you!

Index

A

arrays
  declaring 35

B

break conditions 184
breakpoints
  about 183
  activating 183, 184

C

C/AL code
  XMLports, running from 124
C/AL function
  data, exporting from 125, 126
C/AL
  XML import 127
callstack 186
card pages
  about 78
  creating 79
Client/Server Integrated Development Environment
    (C/SIDE)
  about 17
  application objects 18
  Hello World example 20
  schema synchronization options 57
code coverage
  capturing 188, 190
Codeunit variables 46
Codeunit
  compiling 27
  functions, calling from 46, 48, 49
compilation errors
  handling 28, 29
condition

removing 186
conditional breakpoints
  about 185
  setting 185
CSV files
  data, importing from 107, 108, 110
custom events
  publishing 145

D

data items
  based on temporary tables 176, 177, 178, 179
data
  exporting, from C/AL function 125, 126
  importing, from CSV files 107, 108, 110
  importing, from XML files 111, 112, 113
database trigger events 135, 136, 137, 138, 139,
    140, 141
debugger
  activating 181, 182
default lookup
  configuring 61
default pages
  configuring, for tables 60
drilldown pages
  configuring 61
DrillDowns
  implementing 94, 95
Dynamics NAV Development Shell
  objects, managing 23, 24, 25

E

error handling 27
event publisher function 146, 147
events
  raising 147

F

FactBox subpages 85, 86, 88
field calculation formula
  configuring 66, 67
field
  adding, to page 68
FieldClass
  modifying 65
FieldDelimiter 109
FieldSeparator 109
filtered table relationship
  setting up 63
function parameters 30
function return value 30, 32
functions
  calling 30
  calling, from Codeunits 46, 48, 49
  declaring 29
  parameters, adding to 31

G

global variables 37, 38

I

integration events 130, 131, 132, 133, 134
interactive reports 174, 175
Internet Information Services (IIS) 8

L

list page
  about 80
  creating, page wizard used 60, 61
ListPart subpage 82, 83, 84
local variables 33, 34
lookups 94

M

manual event subscription 149, 150, 152, 153
menu item
  properties 104
Menu suite 100, 102
Microsoft Management Console (MMC)
  NAV server configuration, managing 10
  NAV server instance, creating 10, 12

server settings, modifying 13

N

NAV Administration Shell
  NAV installation, managing 15
  NAV Server instance, creating 15
  NAV server, managing 16
NAV development environment
  installing 8
  license information 10
  setup configuration 8, 9
NAV installation
  managing, with NAV Administration Shell 15
NAV object types
  Codeunit 19
  MenuSuite 19
  Page 19
  Query 19
  Report 19
  Table 19
  XMLport 19
NAV objects
  deploying 21
  exporting 21
NAV server configuration
  managing, with Microsoft Management Console (MMC) 10
NAV server instance
  creating, with Microsoft Management Console (MMC) 10, 12
  creating, with NAV Administration Shell 15
NAV server
  managing, with NAV Administration Shell 16
  TCP ports 12

O

Object Designer
  about 17
  objects, running from 21
objects
  managing, with Dynamics NAV Development Shell 23, 24, 25

P

page action designer 96, 97, 98, 99
page creation wizard
    about 78
    card pages 78, 79
    list pages 80
page triggers
    about 90, 91
    using 92
page wizard
    used, for creating list page 60, 61
page
    field, adding to 68
parameters
    adding, to functions 31
primary keys
    defining 58

R

RDLC expressions 172, 173
Rec global variable 73
record variables 41
records
    filtering 43, 44
    inserting 45
    modifying 45
RecordSeparator 110
recordset
    iterating over 41, 42
report dataset
    preparing 155, 156, 157, 159
Report Definition Language Client Side (RDLC)
    160
report layout
    data output, formatting 165, 166
    design 160, 161, 162, 164, 165
    modeling 159
report request page
    designing 171
report triggers 167, 168, 169
request page
    designing 121, 122, 123
Role Tailored Client
    connecting, to test server 14

S

secondary indexes 60
server settings
    modifying, with Microsoft Management Console
        (MMC) 13
SQL Server
    table metadata, synchronizing 56, 57
syntax error highlighting 29

T

table data
    exporting 119, 120
table indexes 59
table metadata
    synchronizing, with SQL Server 56, 57
table relations
    about 63
    setting up 62
table structure
    designing 53
table triggers
    about 69, 71, 72
    example 70
tables
    creating 54, 55
    default pages, configuring for 60
TableSeparator 110
text constants 50

U

UI events 142, 143, 144, 145

V

variable properties 35
variable scope 33
variables
    about 186, 187, 188
    declaring 33
    global variables 37, 38
    local variables 33, 34
    passing, by reference 40
    passing, by value 38
    record variables 41

W

watches 186, 187
Windows Management Instrumentation (WMI) 16

X

XML files
  data, importing from 111, 112, 113

XML import
  in C/AL 127
XmlDocument variable
  declaring 46, 47
XMLport Designer 108
XMLport triggers 113, 114, 115, 117, 118
XMLports
  running, from C/AL code 124
xRec global variable 73

www.ingramcontent.com/pod-product-compliance
Lightning Source LLC
Chambersburg PA
CBHW080527060326
40690CB00022B/5046